SECRETS TO A
SUCCESSFUL
EVICTION

FOR LANDLORDS AND RENTAL PROPERTY MANAGERS:

THE COMPLETE GUIDE TO EVICTING TENANTS LEGALLY AND QUICKLY

BY CAROLYN GIBSON

SECRETS TO A SUCCESSFUL EVICTION FOR LANDLORDS AND RENTAL PROPERTY MANAGERS: THE COMPLETE GUIDE TO EVICTING TENANTS LEGALLY AND QUICKLY

Copyright © 2008 by Atlantic Publishing Group, Inc.
1405 SW 6th Ave. • Ocala, Florida 34471 • 800-814-1132 • 352-622-1875—Fax
Web site: www.atlantic-pub.com • E-mail: sales@atlantic-pub.com
SAN Number: 268-1250

ISBN-13: 978-1-60138-272-6   ISBN-10: 1-60138-272-3

Library of Congress Cataloging-in-Publication Data

Gibson, Carolyn, 1953-
  Secrets to a successful eviction for landlords and rental property managers : the complete guide to evicting tenants legally and quickly / By Carolyn Gibson.
      p. cm.
  Includes bibliographical references and index.
  ISBN-13: 978-1-60138-272-6 (alk. paper)
  ISBN-10: 1-60138-272-3 (alk. paper)
  1. Eviction--United States. 2. Landlord and tenant--United States. 3. Leases--United States. I. Title.

  KF590.G53 2008
  346.7304'34--dc22
                              2008014393

INTERIOR LAYOUT DESIGN: Vickie Taylor • vtaylor@atlantic-pub.com
PROJECT MANAGER: Angela Adams • aadams@atlantic-pub.com

Printed in the United States

Printed on Recycled Paper

We recently lost our beloved pet "Bear," who was not only our best and dearest friend, but also the "Vice President of Sunshine" here at Atlantic Publishing. He did not receive a salary but worked tirelessly 24 hours a day to please his parents. Bear was a rescue dog that turned around and showered myself, my wife Sherri, his grandparents Jean, Bob and Nancy and every person and animal he met (maybe not rabbits) with friendship and love. He made a lot of people smile every day.

We wanted you to know that a portion of the profits of this book will be donated to The Humane Society of the United States.

— *Douglas & Sherri Brown*

THE HUMANE SOCIETY
OF THE UNITED STATES ©

The human-animal bond is as old as human history. We cherish our animal companions for their unconditional affection and acceptance. We feel a thrill when we glimpse wild creatures in their natural habitat or in our own backyard.

Unfortunately, the human-animal bond has at times been weakened. Humans have exploited some animal species to the point of extinction.

The Humane Society of the United States makes a difference in the lives of animals here at home and worldwide. The HSUS is dedicated to creating a world where our relationship with animals is guided by compassion. We seek a truly humane society in which animals are respected for their intrinsic value and where the human-animal bond is strong.

Want to help animals? We have plenty of suggestions. Adopt a pet from a local shelter, or join The Humane Society and be a part of our work to help companion animals and wildlife. You will be funding our educational, legislative, investigative, and outreach projects in the U.S. and across the globe.

Or perhaps you'd like to make a memorial donation in honor of a pet, friend, or relative? You can through our Kindred Spirits program. If you'd like to contribute in a more structured way, our Planned Giving Office has suggestions about estate planning, annuities, and even gifts of stock that avoid capital gains taxes.

Maybe you have land that you would like to preserve as a lasting habitat for wildlife. Our Wildlife Land Trust can help you. Perhaps the land you want to share is a backyard — that's enough. Our Urban Wildlife Sanctuary Program will show you how to create a habitat for your wild neighbors.

So you see, it's easy to help animals, and The HSUS is here to help.

The Humane Society of the United States
2100 L Street NW
Washington, DC 20037
202-452-1100
www.hsus.org

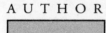

AUTHOR

DEDICATION

This book is dedicated to the memory of my father,
Mose Gibson, the first landlord I knew.

My father was a good man — friendly to all, fair but firm with his
tenants. He had a good sense of humor, loved to hunt
and fish and was a damn good house painter.

AUTHOR

ACKNOWLEDGEMENTS

This book was written in response to all the homeowners who asked me to write about eviction. Because of their questions, concerns, and encouragement at classes I taught, at seminars and on my Web site, I realized that a book solely on the eviction process was needed.

Then there are those who cheered me on, gave advice, information, and support and told me of their confidence in me:

I would like to thank Douglas Brown (President) and Angela Adams (Managing Editor) of Atlantic Publishing Company for their belief in my writing abilities and this book subject.

Kimberly A. Blair, my niece and an excellent property manager.

Elaine Gibson, my sister, who kept me working and focused on the book in a healthy way.

Mary E. Gibson, my mother and my best fan.

Charles S. Mancuso, Esq., the best housing attorney I know.

Barbara St. Claire Post, who helped me organize my thoughts when so much information about the eviction process had my head spinning around.

CONTENTS

FOREWORD

By Glenn L. French, CPM® Emeritus

I have had the pleasure of knowing Carolyn Gibson for more than 30 years. As Certified Property Managers®, we have attended more than our share of conferences and seminars that were focused on the best ways to manage income property to its highest and best use.

When she told me that she was considering writing a book on evictions, I was intrigued as to how she would approach the subject. During my career, a major segment of it has been devoted to turning around underperforming properties, and I know evictions are integral to that process. When she asked that I write a short introduction to her book, it provided the opportunity for me to give a testimonial regarding the knowledge, experience, and credentials she brings to the real estate management industry.

Long ago, I determined that good tenants adhere to a certain value system: they pay their rent timely, they do not damage the property, and they do not infringe on the rights of other tenants. If a property has been neglected for a substantial period, a considerable portion of the tenancy may not adhere to these simple but essential values. When evictions become necessary, it is critically important that the homeowner and real estate manager understand the eviction process definitively. Not pursuing timely evictions may be the quickest way to earn a property a distressed, troubled, poorly performing, or other negative label associated with mismanagement.

Although much of the process may be transparent, the tangential issues remain of residents leaving due to tenants who have already have had eviction papers served but not executed. How do we keep good residents from leaving while these residents in transitory status continue to occupy the property? These answers are needed in our industry.

Carolyn Gibson is a professional who has earned the respect of her fellow property managers nationally. Early in her career, she managed high-risk tenants and troubled scattered site properties, as well as maintenance and cleaning crews. She earned a reputation for being a first-class administrator and supervisor with the respect of her superiors, staff, and residents.

Her book is impressive and reflects her vast experience managing residential properties. Although Carolyn's emphasis is rightly on preventing evictions, she outlines the necessary sense of urgency of an eviction, when it is prudent and preferable for a homeowner to conduct his or her own eviction case, and when hiring an attorney is a better choice.

Her approach to showing how certain prevention techniques can avoid evictions is of great benefit. But when eviction is the prudent choice, she clearly indicates how the eviction should proceed.

If you need information on the eviction process outlined in a concise and plain-English manner, this book will fulfill that need.

Glenn L. French, CPM® Emeritus is the president of Raleigh, North Carolina-based G. L. French & Associates, Inc., a real estate management consulting firm. Currently, the company is actively involved with the HUD's transitioning of public housing agencies to an asset-management model of operations. A member of the Institute of Real Estate Management (IREM®) for more than 30 years, he serves on its national faculty as a dean. He is the recipient of the Louise and Y. T. Lum Award from the IREM Foundation for his many contributions to the real estate management industry and also has received the Foundation's Lloyd Hanford Sr. Distinguished Faculty Award for teaching excellence. Mr. French is also a member of the national faculty of NeighborWorks America.

1   WHY EVICT YOUR TENANT?

An eviction is a lawsuit filed by one party (homeowner, agency, or housing authority) against another (tenant, company, or agency) in order to repossess a specific piece of real estate property. In order for an eviction to be legal, there must be a request committed to written form to either cure the rent arrears or to move out of the apartment. The tenant is allowed his or her day in court to give good reason for the legal action not to take place. Both sides are heard and tried in court by a judge or jury. The case is completed after receipt of a formal permission order from the local or state judicial court, or the landlord can lose the case based on some missing items or required evidence. The landlord would then have to start the eviction process over from the beginning.

Real estate, despite market highs and lows, is still a good buy. Rental income property is a better buy if you need income to defray your mortgage and other property expenses. However, there might come a time when the owner will have to evict the tenant from the property. It is the inevitable fact of owning rental income property. A real estate eviction is a fact of business that will never go away.

Homeowners occupy most residential real estate. According to a report of the first quarter 2008 U.S. Census Bureau, small homeowners comprise more than 67 percent of the U.S. population. In 2007, 4.34 million homes were purchased. Of those properties, 70 percent were bought as a source of rental income.[1] (See Bibliography for resources references.)

The real estate market is cyclical. The number of renting households is now more than 35 million, one-third of all U.S. households.[2] Home buyers increasingly need to purchase a house with rental income attached to have a financial cushion. Or you may hold on to a property for the extra income after purchasing a new one. If the market is low and you cannot get the right price for your home, you can rent it out until the housing market improves. Small real estate investors, forced to hold on to their properties longer than usual, might at some point find themselves as new landlords.

Owning rental income property does come with a price. One of the most complicated, expensive, frustrating, and at times, antagonistic aspects of owning property is the legal eviction process. An eviction occurs often when a tenant who fails to pay the rent or is having a negative or detrimental impact on your rental property. Eviction is the method used when you ask your tenant to move out of your apartment and the tenant stays. This legal process is the most objective and effective way of reclaiming your apartment, house, or building from a tenant who has violated your lease, rules, property, government laws, or other tenants in the building.

When you evict a person or family, you cannot just knock on the tenant's door and say, "Get out by Friday." There are rules of law and decorum that must be followed. You and your tenant agree to abide by specific guidelines, outlined in the lease. When there is no agreement, and the tenant decides to stay in your apartment and not pay the rent or continues to damage the property, that situation could tie up your finances for months.

A homeowner must have formal, written permission from a civil or housing court judge to evict a person or family. The court also dictates in what manner you may evict and in what time period. The primary reason for the eviction legal process stems from the fact that your priorities and those of your tenant are no longer compatible. Some owners are assertive in taking legal action, while others fear or try to avoid using the legal process. You need to take eviction action:

- When the tenant has not paid the rent as charged

- When you have to go into your personal or savings funds to pay the mortgage instead of being able to use the rent money

- When you are unable to pay your credit card and other bills or pay the mortgage

- When the tenant refuses to change destructive behavior affecting the property or other tenants

- When the tenant is unable to control or change negative or illegal behavior or that of his or her family, friends, or visitors to the apartment

- When your valuable tenants start to move out because of your trouble tenant

- When you terminate the lease for good cause and the tenant stays in the apartment

- When everything else has failed to get the tenant to cooperate and respect your property and other tenants

As a Certified Property Manager®, I have observed many homeowners in housing court. Tired, confused, and angry owners spend valuable court time trying to rectify a situation that perhaps could have been avoided.[3] Sometimes, they waited too long to start their legal action and appear desperate and unorganized in court. They do not have a navigation map of the eviction or court process. They make mistakes, and some lawsuits do not go in their favor. This is a tragedy, especially for elderly homeowners, who, at their stage of life, do not need the extra frustration of working through a learning curve to deal with a bad tenant.

Homeowners want to know the best and fastest way to evict a tenant. There is not one way to make it happen best or fast. I do not even think it needs to happen at all if certain ground rules and policies are developed and firmly and consistently carried out with the tenant when they are supposed to be, before it is too late to recover. Evictions can either be timely or lengthy, depending on your preparation time and the type of court case. The goal is to win the first time in court.

Eviction prevention begins at the tenant selection stage. A homeowner might do a good job of renting vacant apartments to tenants, but there will be times when the selection process fails. The tenant becomes intolerable to the homeowner for whatever reason. You try to resolve the problem with reason, threats, or a simple request to vacate the unit. Nothing seems to work. The choice is either to hire a lawyer at great expense, or try to do the eviction on your own.

Especially for first-time homeowners, some basic information on important rules of law and the landlord/tenant relationship is critical. If you are going through tough financial times because of a delinquent or destructive tenant, do not throw the keys back to the bank just yet. Owners need to know what they can and cannot do to evict a tenant and the best ways to prepare to win an eviction.

A homeowner with rental income should treat the real estate property as a serious business investment. You paid money to a bank or mortgage company with a 20- or 30-year financial commitment. The bank expects you to pay the monthly mortgage on time and to maintain, if not increase, the value of the property over that time. Your property has income and expenses that will be reported to the IRS every year. As long as that mutual agreement is sustained, you are left alone by the bank to run your business, the real estate asset, as you see fit.

Tenants, as well as owners, have rights. You agree to allow a tenant to occupy your property in exchange for a specific amount of money and a commitment to maintain the value of the unit. When a tenant violates the lease agreement, the owner has the right to ask the tenant to give back the apartment.

You are expected to operate your property in the confines of local, state, and federal laws and ordinances. Housing and landlord/tenant laws are different from state to state. Every homeowner with tenants, even if they are friends or relatives, should research these laws. Alternatively, have an experienced real estate attorney give you legal advice based on the laws in your state or the state where the property is located. If you choose to hire an attorney, do it before you start any eviction action. As the owner of a business investment, it is in your best interest to become an informed real estate owner or investor.

Eviction has long-term advantages and disadvantages. When you file an eviction case that goes full circle, your tenant will have a blemish on his or her credit and on public record. The case may create a homelessness situation. A completed eviction allows other homeowners who do their research to see that this tenant has a negative history with a landlord.

On the positive side, you will develop experience in going through the eviction process, send a message to your other tenants that you are serious regarding rent and behavior, and reclaim your real estate space to put another tenant who is more stable.

Secrets to a Successful Eviction is not meant to answer or address your legal questions, nor will it address every possible situation. This book will not address evictions due to condominium conversion, Section 8 (federally subsidized housing) conversion to market rents, commercial real estate, college dormitories, or evictions due to foreclosure by a bank or mortgage company. Those evictions are well represented by a multitude of good books and by attorneys experienced in those types of cases.

You will receive information on how to document tenant problems and other necessary information in preparation for a residential eviction. You will also learn what you need to know and do as a homeowner before you decide whether to take a tenant to court. There will be a series of recommendations and plans of action, as well as information on adhering to and using the law to evict a resident from your home or investment.

If you have just bought a house in the last six months, you might not have the money to hire an attorney. There are landlords who will try an eviction case without legal counsel because of financial issues or because they believe that the process can be completed without complications. If you are not confident that you can or want to do your own eviction, hire a good real estate attorney.

THE COST OF EVICTION

The 2004 Census Bureau reported that for 33.7 percent of American homeowners, income from rent was the main reason for purchasing rental income property. Monthly rent and timely payments are key elements of success for a homeowner. If you depend on the rent to help cover the mortgage each month and the tenant fails to pay it or consistently pays it late, you could go into foreclosure. Your credit score would be subsequently lowered.

One alternative to nonpayment of rent is to use your own income to make up the difference, but if you had that kind of money, you would not have bought a rental income property. The longer the tenant does not pay, the further into your pocket you must go to pay the mortgage. This might leave your other bills unpaid, shoving you into possible bankruptcy.

Bank or mortgage company foreclosure happens after you run out of money. If you knew how to get the tenant back on a paying basis or how to remove that tenant and get one who could pay the rent, then you would have a real estate business that could pay its own bills. The solution is to get your tenant to pay the rent before you run out of savings.

According to **www.Bankruptcyhome.com** on its 2006 Web site, inability to pay the mortgage or insufficient time to make up missed payments is one of the top three reasons why homeowners file for bankruptcy. The AARP Bulletin (**www.aarp.org**) states in its July/August 2007 issue that personal bankruptcy filings from 1994 to 2002 increased by 45.8 percent among people age 55 and over. Processing a timely eviction to replace your current tenant with a stable, rent-paying tenant can help bring in the income to keep your home.

This book will address the basics of evicting a tenant in the most fair, efficient, unbiased, and common sense ways. At the same time, there is a time and a place to hire the services of a good, experienced real estate or housing attorney. You will have a time when the eviction case will be difficult, mainly because of complicated eviction laws in your state. Hire an attorney if the tenant hires an attorney. Tenants have also been encouraged to stay abreast of the eviction laws in order to protect themselves from unscrupulous landlords. Many of them do quite well in eviction court on their own.

When you lose an eviction case and have to start all over because you were unaware of a new law or judicial policy, you cost yourself money, time, and the aggravation of seeing your tenant remain in your apartment. Most of that time, the tenant will not pay rent until you file the new court case. Chapter 16 shows how a lawyer can help you navigate a complicated eviction.

Because of the mindset of the average homeowner and tenant, and because I have seen so many of the same habits displayed over many years of managing residential property, some critical parts of the eviction processed may be emphasized in more than one chapter.

EVICTION MOVE-OUT EXPENSES

If every tenant lived in your apartment the way you wanted, there would be no need for eviction. If every tenant were able to stay fully employed, married forever, and had obedient, well-mannered children, family, and friends and no addictions, you would have little to worry about. You could collect your rent each month, pay your mortgage and other property bills, and maintain your building or house in good condition. You might even be able to make a profit from your real estate investment.

However, there might come a day when the bliss of home ownership will fall to the unfortunate, if not inevitable, misery caused by tenant-related problems. Your tenant might lose his or her job and have to live off unemployment for months before finding another job paying at or near what was once earned. Your tenant might lose a spouse to a divorce or separation, leaving the remaining spouse to pay the rent alone. There could come a time when even the most pious, honest, stable, or reliable tenant could fall to alcohol or illegal drug use. Any or all of these circumstances could lead to a need to file for an eviction.

Tenant eviction is a serious matter. Your actions could make the tenant a homeless person or family for a long time. Even a working person or family could have difficulty obtaining housing in the time period of an eviction. As a business owner, you should attempt to use preventive approaches before deciding that a lawsuit is the only way to solve your problem with a tenant.

The residential eviction process is costly, even if you do it all yourself. You will lose time, money, and the repairs and painting you completed on the apartment, and you will have added frustration, anger, and sometimes, even desperation during the process.   21

Here is an example of what can be lost financially during and after the course of an eviction lawsuit. Let us look at an average nonpayment of rent eviction case, completed without the benefit of an attorney[4]:

WHAT CAN BE FINANCIALLY LOST	
First month's nonpayment of rent [5]	$763
First notice to quit — constable service	$50
Constable fee (court notice)	$50
Summary process court fee	$150
Lost landlord salary for day in court [6]	$140
Second month's rent	$763
Constable writ of possession notice served	$50
Moving truck, movers, and warehouse [7]	$1,500
Change locks, paint, and repair unit	$1,000
Third month's rent	$763
Tenant selection process	$150
Security deposit kept by landlord	$(763)
Minimal estimated total expenses to evict a tenant	$4,616

Again, this is without attorney expenses. The costs in your state may be more or less than these figures, but the point is made. These numbers are one reason why prevention is much better than eviction. Sometimes, it is cheaper to keep a tenant if you can find a mutual way to work things out.

Therefore, given the cost of an eviction, the time, and, invariably, the aggravation of taking legal action, the biggest question to ask yourself before you start the eviction process should not be, "How fast can I get this tenant out of my apartment?" The question to ask should be, "What will happen to my property if I do not evict?" There will come a time when talking is over and it is time to take action against your tenant. When you are at your wit's end with a delinquent or destructive tenant, if you find you have to evict your friend or relative, remember — you do not evict a tenant; a tenant evicts him or herself by taking or avoiding action(s) that subsequently will cause you to have to act in response.

2 LANDLORD POLICIES THAT MANAGE TENANT EVICTIONS

You have invested plenty of money purchasing your piece of real estate. You need methods and operational procedures to maintain your investment to its highest and best use. The first time you exchange space in your building or house for money (rent), you conduct a business transaction.

Where and when necessary, I will discuss eviction prevention. There will always be situations beyond your control that will have a financial impact on you and your real estate investment. Tenant divorces, loss of employment, or disabling injuries are only some of the reasons that you might have to evict for nonpayment of rent. A tenant dealing drugs from the apartment, frequent loud parties, and vandalism of your building or appliances are other reasons you might have to evict.

Some evictions begin before you even give the keys to the new tenant. How you move your tenant into your real estate investment could affect the way your tenant-landlord relationship will evolve. Therefore, you should take as much care in renting out your vacant apartment as you will have to if you have to evict the tenant.

You should have policies in addition to your lease that you implement in order to keep your investment maintained.

You should also take the time to read and research the local, state, and federal laws and ordinances in the location of your property. Owning property without knowing how to manage your investment is like filing income taxes without knowing the tax rates and updated laws for the year. Take the time to review, purchase, and read the real estate management books in the Appendix so you can be an informed homeowner.

Your business policies should begin with a selection process to choose the kind of tenant that you want to live in your building; they continue with your lease. This document should cover your expectations of your tenant, how you want the tenant to behave in your apartment, and when, how, and where the rent should be paid. A lease is the best way to avoid confusion or potential future denial about your rules by the tenant.

Every homeowner should use a written lease, especially timid homeowners, to avoid dealing with an assertive or aggressive tenant. If you are new to the rental process, there are tenants who can be intimidating or are expert in "getting over" on a new or timid landlord. By using a lease, you can quote chapter and verse any violation to that kind of tenant, rather than allow a debate over your policies and what you said versus what you meant to say. You can also add your own policies, or lease addenda, to the master lease. If you do not want pets in the apartment, add it to the lease. If you allow a cosigner, add a cosigner agreement to the lease.

If you choose not to use a lease, you create a month-to-month tenancy. The tenant should still know your expectations and policies regarding payment of rent and the manner of behavior in your apartment. It is always best to commit your policies in writing. It keeps everyone honest, and no one has to depend on memory as to what was said or understood.

Do a move-in apartment inspection with the tenant before the tenant gets the keys. There might come a time when you will have to charge the tenant for damages to your apartment. When the tenant moves out, you will have to assess — and may keep a portion of the security deposit to cover — tenant damages. You have to have a beginning point in time to confirm what was damaged and the condition of the unit when the tenant moved in.

If you charge last month's rent and a security deposit, how much of that rent money will be returned to your tenant might depend on your move-in apartment inspection. The tenant should sign the completed move-in inspection form at the same time as the lease. If your move-out apartment inspection shows considerable damage (different from wear and tear) to your apartment, you will have the right to keep a portion of the security deposit to make those repairs.

Always charge a fair market rent, even if your mortgage is paid up, even to friends or relatives. In some states, if a tenant is allowed to occupy a piece of property rent-free for a period of years undisturbed, that person could inherit the property under state homesteading laws. Tenants will respect your property more if you charge a rent that is close to the local rents in the neighborhood.

Rent collection must be a priority for you. It must become a habit, where you expect the rent to come in at the same time every month. You should always collect the rent as if you are deeply in debt and need the money. In this way, paying the rent will become a priority for your tenant.

You do not do your tenant a favor by failing to adhere to a strict rent payment policy. The more rent the tenant owes after the first month, the harder it will be for the tenant to pay as time goes on. Once you start the eviction process, it sends the message that you want your rent on time, or the tenant will face legal action.

Be punctual about collecting rent. You let your tenant know that rent is not important to you when you fail to collect it on time each month. Failure to be consistent in collecting rent will cost you credibility with your tenants. The tenant's attitude could soon develop to, "Oh she doesn't mind if I'm a few days late, as long as she gets it." Left unchecked, that kind of attitude could be the beginning of your getting the rent on the last day of the month instead of the first.

RENT PAYMENT POLICIES

You need to establish or have a rent collection policy for each tenant. It should be the same policy for everyone, regardless of whether the tenant is related to you. When or if the tenant stops paying the rent, you will explain your rent collection policies to the judge and why you are taking legal action. Your policies should be based on your property expenses, research, and knowledge of the landlord/tenant laws in your state.

1. Your first rent payment policy should be to make rent due on the first day of each month and considered late on the second. This policy is often the first one violated, with or without a lease. Every tenant and many landlords think there is a mandatory "grace period" where rent is concerned. Unless your lease says so, there is no "grace period."

2. Start your eviction case in the same month that the rent is due. Do not anticipate that the rent will be paid later in the month, especially if the tenant has not contacted you and told you the rent will be late. The earlier you start the eviction process, the less time will pass before you either get all of your rent or vacate the apartment for a new tenant.

3. If you want to give your tenant time to cash or deposit a paycheck, you should simply state in the lease that rent is due on the third or fifth day of each month. But to say that rent is due on the first, then do nothing if it does not get paid until the fifth each month is fooling no one. By allowing a tenant to pay on a different day other than what the lease says, it could also change your lease. If your tenant suddenly begins to pay on the tenth of every month and you accept it on the tenth of every month and deposit it, you have allowed the tenant, by your behavior, to set a different rent payment day. To avoid this, write the tenant a letter stating that you have received the rent late, and remind him or her that the rent is still due on the first and considered late on the second day of each month.

4. If you live in the building with your tenants, tell them they can slip the rent in an envelope under the door. If you rent apartments other than where you live, invest in a post office box. You might have a good relationship now, but if and when you have to evict a tenant, your home could become the target of anger and retaliation. Your automobile tires could get slashed, your windows broken, your car spray-painted, or threatening

notes might be left in the hallway. By using a post office box, you remove yourself as a potential target.

5. A landlord or property manager should never accept cash for a rent payment. Cash can get mingled with your personal funds. You could take the cash and forget to send a receipt. Later in court, without a record, there will be conflict about what monies were paid.

   Once you start the eviction process, accept only a certified check or money order. In this way, you can write on the check that you are not accepting the payment as rent but for use and occupancy only, reserving all your legal rights. You can copy the payment as proof to the judge. More on this procedure will be addressed later in the book.

6. Never accept a third-party check. Have the tenant cash the check, then get a money order or certified check for you. It is tough enough getting the rent from your own tenant. You do not need to add a third party to the mix. Check with your state laws to see if a rent payment from the cosigner on the lease is valid.

An "As Is" Policy Might Hurt Your Case

You rented your apartment to a young man "as is," that is, without making minor repairs or painting before you leased it out. He recently relocated into the area and needed a place to live in a good location. Knowing you were looking for a good tenant, your brother referred him to you. The applicant looked at several apartments, and even though the rent was a little high, he decided to lease your unit.

Over a period of months or a year, the tenant ultimately gets the apartment looking beautiful. He made all the necessary repairs, installed carpet in the living room and bedroom, and re-tiled the kitchen floor. He painted the apartment with two coats in every room.

When you make your tenant fix up his own apartment, never believe he is happy with that situation. He might feel a little better if you give him a month's free rent in exchange for the repairs, but the tenant might infer that you have made him a reluctant investor of some sort. This might not be what you are trying to do, but in the tenant's mind, it is what you did. You had the tenant renovate your real estate investment as a condition of occupancy. Even if he recognized that he was in a bind and you were kind enough to rent to him, in his gut, he will still feel you took advantage of him.

Upon lease renewal, you give the tenant a rent increase of $100 per month. You figure the apartment is in much better shape than it was a year ago and worth more rent, but the tenant knows the reason why the apartment has increased in value is because he did the work. He made the initial investment, and now you, the landlord, will reap the benefits.

You can see where the tenant might have a negative attitude about your raising the rent. You are trying to take the benefit of his investment in the property to increase your profit margin at his expense. This tenant might stay, not so much because he has nowhere else to go, but because of his investment in the apartment.

If there comes a time when you have to evict the tenant for nonpayment of rent, your "as is" policy may come into question.

Do not think the tenant will not mention to the judge that you made him fix up the apartment. The extra expenses to paint and repair the apartment always come into question when a tenant is being evicted. The tenant will imply that you should have compensated him for the repairs and paint job.

There are other scenarios to consider. When the tenant moves out, he might take his investment with him, removing the carpet from the floor and the ceiling fans from the ceilings. He might stay in the apartment without paying the rent for the last month before he moves out. He also might not care about getting the security deposit back. You can send the initial eviction notice to quit, but he might be gone before you get to court. This is why landlords now lean toward charging first and last month's rent, plus a security deposit.

3 GOOD COMMUNICATION IS ESSENTIAL

Whe hen you are interviewing candidates for your apartment, the first things you should communicate are your expectations from your tenant. At that time, you should make it clear to every apartment applicant that you expect the rent to be paid on time, you expect a phone call if it will be late, and you want your tenant to have a healthy respect for the apartment and others in the building and strict adherence to the lease. In addition, go over your written building policies with the tenant.

The tenant does not have to accept your rules and regulations. If there will be a conflict, now is the time for the two of you to find it out. Take the time to explain how you want the building and the apartment to be treated. This should be done as part of your interviews with rental applicants. It is one way to ensure that your applicant is clear about his responsibilities, should he be selected for your apartment.

If none of this happened before you moved in your tenant, then there was not good communication between the two of you from the start. There must be a "meeting of the minds." Unless you took the time to read the lease to the tenant and go over each section, do not expect the tenant to do so. At the beginning of a tenancy, the only thing a tenant is thinking about is getting the keys and moving into your apartment.

When your tenant does not respect your expectations, communication again should be attempted. No one in good conscience should start an eviction without at least talking with the tenant about it first. The first action is to have a face-to-face discussion. Tell the tenant which part of the lease is in violation. Talk about how disappointed you are about the situation. Remind your tenant of your initial interview meetings and the expectations you shared about rent and behavior before you turned over the keys. Then inform the tenant of the consequences if the situation does not change for the better. Record the date you had that conversation.

The second action should be in writing. Remind the tenant of the conversation you had in person and inform him that he is in violation of the lease or your policies. Let your tenant know which section of the lease is being broken or which policy is not being respected. The letter or notice should tell the tenant what next steps you will take if the negative behavior does not stop.

An eviction should not come as a surprise to your tenant. The most angry and vicious eviction cases I have observed in court have been the ones where the tenant felt he or she was blindsided by the homeowner. In other words, the tenant thought there was a mutual agreement with the landlord, only to be served with a notice of termination soon after the agreement was made.

Do not be afraid to send your tenant a letter telling him what is wrong. If you have talked to the tenant at least twice about the same problem, a letter is in order. For example, if you have a procedure you use for lease violations, let the tenant know about it. Let the person know that your policy is two verbal warnings, then a letter, then a warning letter, and then the eviction notice. Then stand firm on it. Do not take a neutral position about your plans if the situation does not change for the better.

Even if you have a computer, always keep a hard copy of the original letter in the tenant's file folder. Your computer could crash, or you could lose the disk. If you have to go for eviction, you will need to present a copy of your correspondence to the court.

Maintaining good communication with your tenant could help keep problems from developing before legal action must be taken. When you get into court, it should be clear to the judge that you took the time to work with the tenant before you filed your eviction documents. Good documentation of your actions will go a long way toward helping your case.

Can the Problem Be Worked Out?

You should not wait until you are in a financial crisis situation to address your tenant's nonpayment or late payment of rent. There is nothing wrong in making an inquiry into why you are not getting your rent on time. When you see your tenant or when he comes by to pay the rent, have a brief conversation with him. Realize that the tenant might be experiencing some feelings of panic at not being able to pay the rent. How you approach your tenant, and how he responds, could make the difference between the beginning of a royal battle and the beginning of agreement on a plan of action.

There is a difference between a deadbeat tenant and one having a temporary financial problem, not that your eviction policies and procedures should change. Still, you might be more willing to make a rent payment plan with the good tenant having a temporary hardship than with the deadbeat tenant who has always been late with the rent.

At the same time, do not be gullible when the tenant gives you reasons why the rent is not paid or will be late. You will hear many good reasons for the rent problem. You will also hear some lies that should not persuade you to change your rent payment policy. Some excuses might be:

- My student loan did not come through.

- I had to take my daughter to the emergency hospital this month.

- I did not get as much of an income tax refund as I expected.

- I had to go to a funeral in another state.

- My wife (husband, boyfriend, girlfriend) left me last week.

- My paycheck was stolen.

- My roommate unexpectedly moved out.

- I had to make car repairs, which took most of my income.

- I spent too much for Christmas.

- We did not know my wife was going to have twins.

Do not wait for the tenant's ship to come in. These excuses do not work with the bank or your mortgage company, and they should not work with you. You cannot say, "My tenant is going through some hard times, so I cannot pay the mortgage this month."

Rules to Follow

There are standard procedures that veteran property managers follow when communicating with a tenant about negative behavior or nonpayment of rent. Knowing when and how to communicate could determine how well the eviction will proceed over the course of time. You own the property. You should present your case to the tenant in a professional manner. Changing or forgetting that you control how your case will be presented will make a rocky eviction.

It is not good to show up at your tenant's apartment unannounced. You would not like it if your tenant showed up at your home to give you a repair complaint. You would rather have that request made over the telephone. Give the tenant the same respect. Call and ask for a convenient time to meet in the next 24 to 48 hours. Tell the tenant what you plan to discuss in non-specific terms. Say you need to talk about the rent or wish to discuss some issues about the building. If you start to talk about the problem over the telephone, there is no reason to meet. That will be the tenant's goal.

Agree on the time and date. Call the tenant before you head out the door. You want to make sure he or she is not going to duck you by not answering the door. If caller ID warns the tenant you are on your way, you would rather know he or she is "not home" before you leave the house.

Sometimes, the communication problem comes from a landlord who has been much too friendly with the tenant. Perhaps they are related or became fast friends when they discovered they had similar interests. If the time arises when it looks as though an eviction is coming, expect the tenant to be angry and feel betrayed. The tenant might feel misled by your behavior and feel that you have changed the nature of the relationship. You might feel betrayed by someone you trusted.

This is a hazard of renting to friends or relatives. The closer you are to one another, the more bitter the eviction that will follow. Expectations are high at the beginning that the tenancy will be a success. Still, things happen, and when you find you must take legal action, expect communication to fall to a new low between the two of you.

Entire families have been known to choose sides when an eviction happens between friends and relatives. Good communications must be often, clear, preferably in writing, and limited to the issue under consideration.

Pick your time to communicate with your tenant. If you meet with the tenant and feel that he or she is under the influence, make an appointment to speak with the tenant on another day. If your tenant is under the influence, his or her personality, tone of voice, and facial expressions will be different, and he or she could become argumentative, verbally abusive, or try to enter your personal space.

There is no hurry to talk to an inebriated or high tenant. If you do, you could find yourself in an unproductive shouting match or a physical confrontation. Just say that you might have arrived at a bad time and ask if you can schedule a meeting to talk on another date.

Make sure the tenant understands what you are trying to say. Do not let an issue escalate into a war because of a misunderstanding. If the tenant's first language is not English, ask the person who helped the tenant fill out the rental application to attend the meeting.

How you talk to your tenant is important. Your attitude should be one of respect. I have seen some verbal brawls happen over the use of a tenant or manager's tone of voice. Always be professional, even if the tenant is not, starts to swear, and tries to enter your personal space. Again, that is a time to back off and tell the tenant you will discuss the matter later.

4 MAINTAIN A RATIONAL APPROACH

Your approach and attitude during the eviction process will have a big impact on how an eviction will go. By the time you have made the decision to evict your tenant, many things have already occurred. Not only will you be frustrated, but you are also going to be angry. You have tried to work with the person or family several times before you came to the conclusion that it was time for the landlord/tenant relationship to come to an end.

After you have received the rent and security deposit and turned over the keys to the apartment, you want to interact with your tenant only once a month, to collect the rent. That may be the only time your tenant wants to see you too, to give you the rent. Most tenants want to be left alone to their apartment; most landlords want to be left alone except when rent time comes around.

Therefore, an eviction is a traumatic experience for both parties. Tempers will flare; stress will exist for the entire period of the lawsuit. Both landlord and tenant will go through a myriad of personality changes as the case progresses. Keeping your cool during the eviction process is important. A cool head and a calm attitude could help prevent you from saying or doing things that could come back and damage you in court.

Look at an impending eviction as a professional rite of passage that every landlord will experience at least once in a lifetime of owning property. It should be done with objectivity and not emotion. You should not want to evict a tenant because you are "tired of looking at him" or because every time the two of you talk, he or she grates on your nerves.

Just because the two of you are in business together does not mean you have to like one another. The tenant, regardless of his or her personal behavior, is helping to pay your mortgage and bills. An eviction is too expensive to use it as a way to get rid of someone who is aggravating to you.

Your tenant is supposed to pay the rent, follow the lease, leave other people alone, obey the law, and keep up the apartment and the common areas. Your responsibility as a homeowner is to collect the rent and use it to pay the property expenses, maintain the property, and make sure everyone follows the lease. This is the extent of your relationship with each other.

1. **Do not expect your tenant to like you.** Owning housing is not a popularity contest. You are the person with whom they have to interact at least once a month to conduct business. Unlike paying the car note or a credit card, the tenant might have to see you to pay the rent. There are tenants who hate to pay rent every month. Do not let their attitude get to you.

2. **Never lose your temper with a tenant.** There will be

times when a tenant will make a request or series of requests that will drive you crazy. A tenant might ask you to replace a $3 kitchen sink stopper. If you are having a bad day, you might say or do something you will later regret. The tenant, to your detriment in court, could repeat that nasty comment said in the heat of anger.

3. **Depending on the reason, an eviction could take weeks, if not months to be completed.** Be prepared to be in this for the long haul. In the meantime, you will still have to interact with your tenant before and throughout the case. It does not make sense to be rude or offensive during that time period. It's too long of a process to spend all of your eviction time angry. Keep your perspective; it is not personal, just business.

4. **During the eviction, try to stay away from the tenant as much as possible.** Keep your perspective about needed repairs and other maintenance items around the property. Do not give the tenant any excuse to avoid paying the rent.

5. **Always document your case well in advance of starting legal action.** Most owners suffer through weeks, if not months, of atrocities with a tenant before making the decision to take legal action. Invariably, when the owner wants to put together the termination letter, there will be examples of those many atrocities left out of the notice due to lack of documentation. Put your observations in writing, and file them in the tenant's folder.

6. **The Appendix contains a sample incident report.** It will allow you to document any and all incidents that

happen at the property and between you and your tenant. This will be a valuable piece of evidence that can be presented to the judge if an eviction gets to court.

7. **Separate your personal life from that of the tenant.** This means that you should keep to your business, which is the management of your property, and out of the tenant's personal business. This could be difficult if you have rented your apartment to a personal friend or relative. If you have, understand that you will have established two distinct relationships, one personal and one business.

For example, your tenant is late every month paying the rent. One month, you notice that the tenant has bought a brand-new car, latest edition, with a sunroof. You become angry that the tenant cannot seem to pay the rent on time each month, but apparently he or she has the money to purchase a new car. You get even angrier at the thought that this tenant may pay the car note on time but will still pay your rent late.

It is none of your business how many cars your tenant buys. It is your business to collect the rent on time each month. If you had been sending an eviction notice each time that the tenant was late paying the rent, perhaps he or she would have made a different decision about prioritizing the bills. Perhaps if you had made rent collection your priority, you would not be in this situation. Keep to your business as a homeowner every month, and what the tenant does personally will not matter much to you in the long run.

Certified Property Manager® Glenn L. French explained his techniques for determining whether his eviction case is ready for court in his book, *Government Assisted Housing: Strategies for Site Managers* (Institute of Real Estate Management). His approach is an example of how a homeowner or property manager should look at an eviction case in a calm, rational manner.

EVICTION TIP

Many successful managers have developed a "sixth sense" regarding decisions that may have legal consequences. This sense — I call it liability consciousness — involves developing a decision-making process that sharpens the site manager's judgment in areas that may increase risk for the property owner and management company. Although there are different approaches to developing this sense, I call mine the "courtroom test."

I use this test to review all the "what-ifs" that come to mind regarding a possible decision. Beginning with the worst-case scenario and working toward more likely consequences, I imagine myself testifying during a trial and answering questions about my actions. I ask myself how my answers would sound to the judge, jury, and courtroom spectators. If my hypothetical answers make me feel uncomfortable, I get more facts before making a decision.

You believe the person who presented herself to you as a stable, quality tenant took advantage of you. You now want to get her out before more harm is done to your apartment. Expect to feel betrayed, but you have to stay calm and be rational.

Not every tenant problem needs to end up as an eviction case. You just spent money processing the application and fixing up the apartment to move in this family. The cost of eviction and getting the apartment back up to renting status will drain your finances. A stern, face-to-face talk with the tenant could help cure these issues.

Reason can go a long way toward avoiding eviction action. Being flexible could resolve some situations. For example, if a tenant becomes unemployed and now gets an unemployment check twice a month instead of a weekly paycheck, are you going to evict because the rent is not paid all at once?

Finally, the attitude of you and your tenant toward the eviction process will, in many ways, determine how well the eviction will go. The rent collection process should not result in an adversarial relationship. It is a business transaction, just like paying a car note every month. As the homeowner, you will have to be tough in order to achieve your goal of getting the rent paid on time and in full every month. That does not mean you have to be brutal, but a firm and consistent attitude and behavior will work to get your point across.

Here is an example of how a poor attitude on either side of the fence could have started an unnecessary eviction case. Mr. King, the homeowner, is frustrated with Ms. Freemont, his tenant of one and a half years. Both the owner and the tenant live in the same three-family house. Mr. King goes upstairs to collect the rent. He knocks on his tenant's door.

> *"Ms. Freemont, I'm here for the rent."*

> *"I do not have the rent today, Mr. King. I can pay you Saturday."*

> *"You said that last week. I need the rent today."*

> *"I do not have the rent today. I am behind in all my bills because my 4-year-old was sick. I can pay you on Saturday."*

> *"I do not have anything to do with your child being*

sick. I'm one of your bills, too. As a matter of fact, I should be the first bill you pay every month. I'm getting sick and tired of running up and down the stairs trying to get the rent out of you every month."

"Well, I'm tired of you chasing me for the rent. You know I pay it every month."

"I know it's late every month. I want the rent on the first of the month, not the 15th or 20th of every month or when you feel like paying it."

"You do not have to be nasty about it, Mr. King. I notice you want your rent on time, but I'm still waiting for my faucet to be fixed after two weeks."

"I would not have to be nasty if I got my rent on time, Ms. Freemont. And, I would be able to make repairs on time, too."

"You're supposed to make repairs whether I pay the rent on time or not. It's your property."

"You're right it's my property. And that means I do not have to keep waiting for my rent every month. I can just put you out and get someone else who pays on time."

"Are you threatening me?"

"No. I'm saying I want my rent on time every month. As a matter of fact, I want it by the fifth of the month from now on."

"Fine. You'll get this month's rent on Saturday. Next month's rent will be on time. I just do not want to be threatened with eviction anymore."

"If you pay the rent by the fifth of the month, we will not have to have this conversation again, Ms. Freemont."

"Fine."

"I'll see you on Saturday."

"No, I'll bring it to you on Saturday."

"That's not necessary. I'll pick it up when I come to fix the faucet. Good-bye."

In this scenario, Mr. King walks away, frustrated and angry that he was not firm enough and still did not get his rent. Ms. Freemont closes the door, angry about being confronted about the rent at her own apartment. However, Mr. King did establish when he wanted his rent to be paid every month, to which Ms. Freemont agreed. By saying exactly what he wanted and expressing his future expectations, Mr. King might avoid a possible eviction.

Both the tenant and the landlord wandered into eviction territory during this meeting — Mr. King, when he "mentioned" a possible eviction, and Ms. Freemont, when she challenged his responsibilities as the landlord. Both had valid points. Each became irritated during the meeting. Each stood his and her ground regarding their rights and responsibilities. In the end, they both agreed to comply with their obligations on a specific date.

5 ENLIST THE PROPER AUTHORITIES

Clearly, it is preferable to avoid the eviction process if you can. Getting the assistance of the local authorities might help prevent an eviction. They have information that could help you to avoid taking legal action. Outside intervention could influence the tenant to improve bad behavior or seek counseling to rectify a nonpayment of rent matter. To that degree, an eviction should be a team effort between you and the authorities you might have to work with over the course of the lawsuit. When you ask for the help of your local authority person, this could become a long-term business relationship. Being cordial will go a long way toward getting cooperation.

FRIENDS AND RELATIVES

Your tenant has been coming into your building over the past two months in an inebriated state. He stumbles into the building several times a week, often late at night. He leaves the strong smell of alcohol in the hallway and tries to talk to your teenage daughter, which she hates. Or, your elderly tenant keeps calling you to say there are elves looking through her bedroom window. When you visit her, you notice the extra large bottle of Listerine on her bedroom floor. She looks disheveled and disoriented.

Pull out your tenant emergency contact information form (see Appendix) and call the tenant's friend or relative. Let the person know that you have been unsuccessfully trying to work with the tenant. Ask him or her to assist by meeting with you to review the problem. Ask the friend or relative to visit the tenant in an attempt to solve the problem before you have to take legal action, but be aware that sometimes this does not work.

LOCAL POLICE OR SHERIFF

Your tenants will not always tell you that the police have been to your property. They think you already know or are afraid to get involved. Go to the police headquarters to get a list of all crimes on your street and surrounding neighborhood for the month. The list is public record. See if there has been criminal activity at your building that the police had to address.

The following agencies can assist with a multitude of building problems. They will work together if any one of these departments is unsuccessful in helping you with your tenant problem.

- Fire department

- Department of Elder Affairs

- Housing Inspection Department

- City hall

City hall often has neighborhood liaisons that work with residents and neighborhood groups at the local level. A representative has the ability to use its authority with city hall officials for faster and more precise action.

The fire and Housing Inspection Departments can enforce building and fire code violations, where the landlord might not have the clout. A tenant is less likely to violate a summons from the fire department to explain why he still has illegal bars on the windows after the owner demanded them removed.

Go see the problem for yourself. If there is drug use, you will not have to wait long in your car before seeing the pattern. Take pictures and notes of your observations by date, time, number of people going in and out of the apartment, and other unusual activity. Take your notes and pictures to the police, preferably the drug enforcement unit.

DRUG UNIT

If you suspect illegal drug activity on your property, do not walk, but run to the police department's drug enforcement unit. If you own or manage more than one unit in a building, a drug problem has the potential of spreading. You have to get the law on your side and let officers know you are not condoning the situation.

Working with the local drug enforcement unit at the police department is the best way to get help with drug activities in your apartment. Take your written, video, and/or photo evidence to it. Ask for increased police surveillance drive-by coverage. The police can set up a sting operation by having someone from the unit try to buy drugs from the apartment.

Whatever the police ask you to do, do it. They might ask you to provide a vacant apartment in the building. They also might ask for a key to the front door in case they have enough evidence to break in and arrest people. If they decide to do that, they will not tell you when it will happen. Loose lips sink ships. The fewer who know what law enforcement activities will happen, the better.

NEIGHBORHOOD WATCH

Do not wait until the neighborhood watch group approaches you with a petition about one of your tenants. Use the group's services to help you. The group carries plenty of clout with the local authorities and can get access to the people who can quickly assess your problem and assist you. Go to Chapter 12 for more information on how a neighborhood watch can be beneficial to your case.

CONSTABLE ASSISTANCE

After you receive your permission to evict, called a writ of possession, you must give the tenant 24 to 48 hours advance notice of the eviction move-out, depending on state law. When you send the constable to serve the tenant, you should also have the constable try to talk the tenant into leaving on his or her own. This is sometimes referred as a "talk out," a last attempt to allow the tenant to move out on his or her own to avoid an eviction on the public record.

This is not harassment or a shakedown. You already have the eviction judgment in your favor and have the notice to evict in hand. What the constable will do is explain to the tenant that moving out is preferable to being evicted.

6 YOUR EVICTION MATERIALS

A s a real estate owner, consider yourself a business professional, and act accordingly. When you rent your vacant apartment for money, this is a business deal. When you collect rent, deposit it, and pay bills with the rent money, you are making business transactions every month.

Every business owner should carry the appropriate tools of the trade. This chapter is to provide you with some of the tools of the trade as a homeowner who rents out space to non-owners. These tools are mandatory if you expect to own your rental income property for a number of years. Like your income tax papers, you should keep these materials available for review for the next three to five years.

Tenant Files

An eviction generates plenty of paper. Learn how to keep a set of tenant files. Paperwork on a tenant is important in an eviction case. Many homeowners do not maintain files on their tenants. Once a tenant is moved in and starts to pay the rent on a regular basis, many homeowners take a sigh of relief, put all the paperwork in a large envelope, and do not think about the tenant again until income tax time.

Whether a tenant has been there a year or ten years, a homeowner should always keep a formal method of recordkeeping on every tenant living in his or her home or houses. Every tenant should have a file folder, where all the information on the tenant is held. Better still is to have one folder per year of occupancy.

You may think spending extra money on file folders and hanging folders is not important, but you will need to be organized when you have to gather property information to give to your income tax preparer. Buy colored file folders for each building.

Do not think of this as extra work but as part of your business. If you own a business, you expect your administrative files to be in order. Your property should receive the same care. Just as you keep all information about your business for its annual audit, your building information must be similarly maintained. Depending upon how you set up your property purchase and whether you file deductions, tenant information is mandatory to your income tax reports.

You must maintain your files monthly and keep them organized in case of an eviction. You do not want to have to search through your files before you can start your case.

RENT CARDS OR COMPUTER FILES

If you do not have a computer, rent cards are a good way to maintain your tenants' rent payments. A catalog from Peachtree Business Forms (see Web site information in the resources area of the Bibliography) can show you several sample rent cards from which you can choose.

If you use a computer software program, such as QuickBooks Pro or TenantPro, to maintain your house and tenant financial records, back it up daily. Never leave your financial program before backing up the data on a disk or CD. The day will come when some piece of hardware will fail or you will lose information during a power surge. Your backup disk should have the latest data on your rent records.

A RENT RECEIPT BOOK

If you are the type of landlord who absolutely insists on taking cash, you must own and use a rent receipt book. It should be a two-part receipt book. The original copy is for the tenant, and the second copy is for your tenant and income-tax records. It is better to have the type of receipt book where the copies stay in the book. You can bring the entire book to court for review.

Sometimes a tenant will say he or she paid cash that was not credited toward the rent. With your trusty rent receipt book, you can prove that you received and recorded every cash transaction. If there is space to write whatever rent balance is still due, put in that information.

You can bring a copy of all the receipts, but the judge would rather see the book. It is one proof of your bookkeeping records and adds credibility to your nonpayment of rent case.

FILE CABINET

You should have made up a file folder for each of your tenants after all the paperwork was finished. This file folder should contain everything you know about the tenant, including the original rental application, verification information, the credit check, employment information, and any other documentation. You need a file for all the work orders completed on your property, filed by building and apartment number. These files will be used over the life of the tenancy.

Keep your paperwork in order. When the day comes that you must pull out incident reports (See Chapter 12), letters, and other documents to show evidence to a judge, you want to have everything in one place. Do not just throw papers in your file cabinet. It should take an hour a week or less to separate and file your building and tenant paperwork. You need to be as dedicated to this process as you are with your mortgage and income tax documents. Much of the information will overlap, saving you time and aggravation if kept organized and in one place.

Eventually, if you own your home long enough, you will have a number of files on your tenants, both current and former. A banker's box is a good place to keep these records. A small, two-drawer file cabinet is better. All information regarding the house or building, repairs, ongoing maintenance, evictions, sales receipts, and anything else that might be relevant should be kept in this cabinet for three to seven years.

Keep your former tenants' information separate from your current tenants'. Most property management companies file their past tenant information in a banker's box and store it in a safe place, free from moisture and mold and available for inspection by themselves, you as their client, the IRS, or their insurance company. Your former tenant information should be filed and available to review for at least three years.

Buying a two- or four-drawer file cabinet is a minimal investment in your property. Filing your building and tenant paperwork in a file cabinet will also go a long way should you decide to sell. The prospective buyer will want to know about the property. Your records could make a sale.

CAMERA

You need to own some type of camera. You will need or want evidence of lease violations or security deposit damages to present to a judge in court. A camera is one of the best ways to tell your tale. A one-time use camera can be processed in hours. A digital camera can produce your pictures immediately, and copies, if you have a computer.

A video camera can be used to record an apartment inspection before, during, and after you move in a tenant. The ability to go through each room and show a panoramic view of your apartment is excellent evidence to use in court.

Take a copy of the current daily newspaper and set it down in every room. Make sure you can see the date of the newspaper to show when the picture was taken. The tenant will not be able to deny that the picture was taken after she moved out, for security deposit purposes. If you forget to put a newspaper down to show the date of inspection, develop it the same day you take the pictures, because this is the date you need.

A note of warning: Be careful not to violate your tenant's right to privacy when taking pictures or videotaping. If the apartment is occupied, take pictures only of things you can see out in the open. If they left things such as a dresser after they moved out, open the drawers to show what they left for you to clean up.

Make an investment in a camera or video camera. Keep a one-time camera in your glove compartment all the time. Do not play it cheap and decide not to take a picture when one may be needed to show why you are evicting your tenant. In every case, make sure that your pictures come out in clear focus. If you cannot make out what you are trying to show as damaged, torn, or vandalized, the judge cannot see it either. Only good, clear pictures will prove your case.

Apartment Inspection Reports

Your tenant may tell the judge that the reason he or she stopped paying the rent is because of the "deplorable conditions" of the unit. Here is where you bring your initial apartment inspection report, which will prove that your apartment was in good condition when you gave the tenant the keys. If you did an initial move-in apartment condition checklist, signed by the tenant, you have a basis to go by if you are evicting your tenant for excessive damages in the unit. If your apartment was initially inspected and approved by the Section 8 inspector, bring that report and all annual inspections to court.

Further, you should have subsequent apartment inspection forms completed during the tenancy. Do an apartment inspection twice a year and have the tenant sign it. Bring your apartment inspection forms with you to court to prove the apartment was in good condition before you started eviction procedures.

CAN AN EVICTION BE AVOIDED?

Most times, if the owner and/or manager can stay on top of a situation, an eviction can be avoided. If you have strong policies and enforce them each time with every violation, tenants will know that you are serious about maintaining your apartments.

When you have policies and do not require compliance with them, when you play favorites or when you let lease violations go unenforced, you should be prepared for an eventual eviction of a tenant. Human nature sometimes demands that we try to see how far we can get away with something, especially if we are told we have to do something specific. We will sometimes go out of our way to test the rule or person. There are tenants who will feel compelled to violate a policy, just to see what you will do about it.

You might be able to work with the tenant in an attempt at preventing a prolonged and costly eviction, but other tenants are watching the scenario play out. When you go out of your way to avoid an eviction, you are telling tenants that your policies and lease are not real, just something they had to sign. You send the message that you will do almost anything to avoid going to court.

There must be a line drawn between being reasonable and being taken advantage of by a tenant. An eviction case should be the homeowner's remedy of last resort. That does not mean you should allow yourself to be used or taken advantage of by your tenant. It means that you should use preventive strategies, consistent lease enforcement, and prompt verbal and written communication with your tenant to avoid the need to file what could become a costly lawsuit.

There are those situations, however, where eviction action is unavoidable. Reasons why an eviction should begin are:

- The rent is not paid for the month by the deadline date.

- The tenant has broken a written rent arrears payment agreement, either with you or the housing court.

- Your other tenants threaten to move out if you do not do something about the person or family creating a nuisance.

- Your property is being severely vandalized by the tenant, tenant's friends or relatives, or visitors of the tenant.

- Your neighbors consistently complain about your tenant and want you to do something about it.

- You strongly suspect or can prove illegal activities are being conducted out of the apartment.

- Your property value is going down because of a shameful reputation of having bad tenants in it.

- Repairs to the property cannot be made due to nonpayment of rent issues.

- You have to come out-of-pocket to pay the mortgage because the tenant is not paying the rent on time every month.

If you cannot take care of the rent collection process every month because you are too timid to ask for the rent or are too accommodating around tenant excuses, you should not own rental property. Alternatively, you should hire a property management company to manage your property. Rent collection should be a simple matter of adhering to your own policies, as given to the tenant before you gave out the apartment key.

7 NONPAYMENT OF RENT EVICTION

P art of the process of making a business decision is to determine whether an eviction is necessary. Consider whether there are other ways of getting all your rent each month without going to court. Also determine whether something specific is going on with your tenant that is temporary or that could be solved with some creativity.

An owner should be self-driven to find an alternative before sending a termination notice. If the tenant has rejected the alternative to termination, then you can appropriately follow through with your eviction.

One should never stop an eviction, once started, until achieving the goal that caused you to begin taking legal action. You can, however, use some preventive measures before the situation gets to the court stage. We will review some of those measures in this chapter and look at some strategies that have worked for me as a property manager.

NONPAYMENT OF RENT

The first time you exchange space in your home (apartment) for money (rent), you have conducted a business transaction.

That makes the rent collection process a business, not a hobby. When your tenant first moves into your apartment, you need to tell him or her that rent is due on the first and late on the second. If your bank gives you a ten-day grace period, you should not give your tenant more than a five-day grace period. Most landlords and rental agents allow a three- to five-day grace period to give the tenant time to cash a paycheck. By law, you do not have to give a grace period.

Always charge a fair market rent. Even if your mortgage is paid, you still need funds to pay the real estate taxes, maintain the property, and pay for major repairs. It is also not wise to avoid an eviction by charging the tenant more rent than he or she can afford to pay.

Evicting a tenant for nonpayment of rent by way of a written notice should stand as the formal method to collect your rent. Rent is owed to you by law and by your lease and should not be considered or treated as the tenant doing you a favor. You want and expect your rent on time, every month. If the tenant cannot pay it, you want the tenant to move out. You will put someone else in the apartment who can pay the rent.

The person or people who signed your lease owe the monthly rent, equally and in total. This means if you have a husband and wife tenancy and the husband loses his job, the total rent is still due. The same pertains with roommates. If one roommate cannot pay the rent for the current month and all three are on the lease, the other two roommates will have to pay for that roommate. They cannot go to you and say they can pay only two-thirds of the rent because one roommate came up short. If a new roommate ever moves in, you should add that person to the lease as an addendum or execute a new lease, making all the roommates responsible for the rent.

HOW TO NOTIFY THE TENANT

You can inform your tenant verbally that the rent is due. You can also tell the tenant that if the rent is not made current by the first of the month, you want him or her to move. However, in many states, a verbal demand is not admissible in court. Without a written notice asking for either the rent or the apartment and legitimate proof that the notice was served on the tenant, it is just a conversation between the two of you.

If you want a tenant to move out of your apartment for nonpayment of rent, it should always be in writing, along with the reason for the eviction. If the tenant owes $1,431.01, all for rent, that amount is what should be on the notice of termination. Itemize the months that are unpaid and how much is due for each month.

Make sure you use the proper form or notification for the request. Many states mandate that you must first terminate the lease and make the request for payment of rent — research your state's eviction laws.

Make sure the names of the tenants are spelled correctly on your notice to quit. If there are two or three leaseholders, all names must be on the eviction notice, and all tenants must be served.

PROOF OF SERVICE

In many states, you must prove in court that your tenant received the notice to quit. The tenant must be advised that you are taking legal action. Making the tenant sign a statement that you asked him or her to move will not work. You could send your notice by certified mail, registered, return receipt requested, but a tenant who knows he or she is behind in the rent might not pick it up. By the time the unopened letter is returned to you, you will have wasted ten days or more.

The best way to serve a tenant is by constable or sheriff. They are legal agents of the state. When they serve the tenant, the judge will consider the tenant duly notified.

I like to request the tenant be served in person. Leaving the notice under the door or on the apartment door is not good proof of service. Tell the constable when the tenant is most likely to be home. The constable can serve the notice on weekends in some states. Give the constable or sheriff a time limit for the service. You want it served immediately after you write it.

WHY DID THE TENANT STOP PAYING?

There is often a good reason why a tenant stops paying the rent. Unemployment is one reason, maybe due to corporate downsizing or a merger. Perhaps the tenant was in a car accident and has been unable to work for six weeks or more. A new divorce and/or child support can seriously drain a bank account. These are some legitimate reasons why rent is sometimes late or not paid, especially if the tenant has little or no savings to carry him or her for a time.

Although valid reasons for nonpayment of the rent might draw sympathy, as a course of business, it cannot be allowed as a reason not to receive payment or to hold off taking legal action.

For example, unemployment is a common reason for a tenant's inability to pay the rent. In 2007, according to the Bureau of Labor Statistics, (**www.bls.gov**) more than seven million people were unemployed. The national average length of time a 2007 worker was unemployed was 17 weeks. An employee can receive unemployment insurance for up to 26 weeks, or 6 months.

If you are a landlord and you have just been told that your tenant has become unemployed, chances are the tenant will spend between five and 17 weeks on unemployment insurance. Let us say your tenant makes 1.5 times the national average annual income of $36,400; he makes $1,050 a week. If the tenant works in Massachusetts, this is good news. The state pays the highest unemployment insurance benefits in the country, at $600 per week as of 2008.[8] The bad news is, the tenant's income went from $54,600 a year to $15,600 in the next six months. Almost half of his income has been cut until he finds another job. If your monthly rent is $763, chances are your tenant will not be able to pay it, unless he has a big savings account.

Sometimes a tenant will stop paying the rent because he or she is waiting for you to do something, such as make apartment repairs. The tenant has asked time and again for a repair to be made, and the landlord has failed to do so. The problem goes on, and for some reason, you have either decided not to do the repair or you do not have the money to do the repair. Either way, not paying the rent is sometimes the only thing that will get a landlord's attention.

Do not take too long to make repairs for your tenants. A response time to a non-emergency should be between 24 to 48 hours. Taking too long, more than two weeks for a non-emergency repair or more than 12 hours for an emergency repair, will frustrate a tenant, especially if it is a regular habit of the landlord not to take repair calls seriously.

If you make promises you do not keep and the tenant has to keep calling to get any repairs done, at some point, the tenant will get tired of begging you to do repairs and will take the only action he or she believes will get your attention. Indifference to a tenant's persistent requests for repairs often signals the beginning of a future eviction case.

Late Payment of Rent

Some homeowners want to evict a tenant who is consistently late paying the rent. This is understandable. After all, the bank or the mortgage company wants its money on time each month. If you get your rent late, that will cause you to pay your mortgage late each month. This will give you a bad credit rating, which you do not want to have happen.

Even if you do not have a mortgage, you can insist that the tenant pay the rent on time. You still have bills to pay on the house, such as the water bill, taxes, and insurance that should be paid by the rent, not out of your pocket. You can evict a tenant, or not renew the lease, based on consistently late rent payments.

You are not doing the tenant a favor by allowing the rent to get in arrears. The longer the tenant goes without paying the rent, the harder it will be to catch up. If the monthly rent is $800 a month, and that rent is allowed to carry into the next month, the tenant will then owe you $1,600. That might be too much money for the tenant to provide at once.

State law determines when rent is considered late before you can take court action. Especially if you do not have a lease, you need to know when the law says the rent is late. Some states have decided that rent is not late until the end of the month has passed.

In the state of Maryland, you can begin the eviction process by the fifth day of the month if the rent has not been paid (called a summary ejection). Eviction filing must be in District Court. If the landlord wins his case, he is allowed to put the tenant's belongings on the sidewalk four days after winning the eviction case and receiving the court eviction approval document.

EVICTION **T I P**

The sheriff or constable must be present at the actual move-out as an officer of the court to supervise the removal of the tenant's belongings. The sheriff or constable is not allowed to do any moving duties, only the landlord. On the date of an eviction, the sheriff will come to the rental unit to order the tenant and everyone inside to leave. It is the landlord or the landlord's employee's responsibility to remove all property from the unit and put it on the public sidewalk.

Once the property is moved from the unit, it is the tenant's responsibility to remove and store. The tenant must remove all belongings before anyone on the street takes anything away.

(Maryland Code, Real Property, Sec 8-401) Adapted from the state landlord/tenant code book.

When the rent is late, take action the same month the rent is due. Even if the tenant sends you nice letters or e-mails about his or her problem, it is still his or her problem. Do not allow a tenant to make their financial problem your mortgage problem. Do not listen to sob stories. If you do, you might have to give your own sob story to your mortgage company and other creditors. They will not be so lenient about waiting for their money.

Three key points:

- When you send the tenant a notice to quit for nonpayment of rent, you must send a copy of the notice to the Section 8 leasing officer for the tenant.

- If you have a cosigner, send a copy of the notice to quit to that person also. That person should know in advance that he or she could be on the hook for the delinquent rent.

- Never believe the tenant will get caught up with the rent with an income tax refund. Neither of you is guaranteed the tenant will get a refund. Continue the eviction.

Rent Increases

The following is not an unusual situation. A homeowner has problems with a tenant, and so she decides to raise the rent to encourage the tenant to move out. The tenant is asking for repairs every time he pays the rent. Or, the tenant is behind in the rent, and the landlord raises the rent to give the tenant the message that he can no longer afford the apartment.

These tactics create difficult eviction situations on a homeowner or property manager. A rent increase is a business decision meant to cover the expenses of the property. It should not be used as a retaliation method or a means to get a tenant to move out without an eviction.

Which of the following most closely resembles your reasoning for raising the rent by $100 or $200 a month, and how was this specific amount decided?

- You have not increased the rent for more than five years.

- You recently installed new porches on the front.

- Expenses to maintain the property have gone up substantially.

- You noticed your tenant bought a new car this year.

- All your neighbors on the street are getting more rent than you are charging.

- You notice how hard it is for people to find an apartment lately, and you think if your tenants cannot pay, someone else will.

Consider the possible ramifications of a rent increase. The tenant is already struggling to pay the rent every month. So, you increase the rent. A judge might find it irritating that you would add a rent increase before or during an eviction case. He or she could inquire into your motive in taking this action at this particular time.

A Retaliation Rent Increase

In the spirit of eviction prevention, let us review retaliation and eviction action. You are entitled to a profit, a return on your real estate investment. Every homeowner should increase the rent at least every two years just to keep up with inflation. Expenses to maintain your investment go up every year, as do taxes, utilities, and other expenses. You are also entitled to raise the rent to keep up with neighborhood market conditions.

However, as discussed above, the amount of your rent increase may be questioned as being too high or too arbitrary. If the economy is doing well and jobs are plentiful, a rent increase might not be a big issue for a tenant. If the economy is bad and unemployment and layoffs are in high numbers, a tenant may fight a rent increase on the basis of not being able to maintain or find a job paying enough to cover the increase in rent.

A large rent increase, when you are sure the tenant cannot afford it, is not a good business decision. It is an eviction in the making. You will incur the cost of evicting your tenant because he cannot keep up with the increase. The tenant could stay in the apartment and challenge the increase in court based on the poor condition of the apartment.

If the two of you have been fighting about apartment, children, or pet issues, a rent increase will bring out all those issues in court. It might appear that you could not or did not want to go to court because your case might be weak. Alternatively, you raised the rent.

In some states, if a judge or jury determines that the eviction was caused by a retaliatory rent increase, you could lose your case. The judge may also fine you for retaliatory practices, up to three times the rent.

PARTIAL RENT PAYMENTS

Sometimes a tenant will send a partial rent payment, rather than not send anything. In most cases, this is an attempt at good will, to show willingness, if not necessarily the ability, to pay the rent. A tenant who sends a partial rent payment often sends a note to go along with it that explains why the rent is not paid in full and when you can expect the balance due.

This does not mean that you should not send a notice to quit on the tenant; you should as a matter of policy. It does mean that you also need to have a conversation with your tenant about what is going on. Partial rent payments might mean the tenant has secured a new job that pays twice a month instead of weekly. The question here is whether you can afford to get the rent twice a month, when your mortgage is due the first of the month.

The tenant wants to pay rent on the first and 15th of the month. If you accept this new payment plan, you will have to start eviction proceedings three days after the first or three days after the 15th of the month. There are some states that say if you collect and deposit a partial rent payment, you have voided your notice to quit and must start the eviction process all over again. Before you begin legal action, find out whether your state allows you to accept partial rent payments during the eviction process.

EVICTION QUIZ — NOT ENOUGH RENT PAID

You gave your tenant-at-will (month-to-month) resident a rent increase notice 60 days ago. You did not hear back from the tenant. The day the new amount is due, the tenant pays you the old rent. The check was slipped under your door while you were at work. You:

a. Give the check back to the tenant, with a note asking for the correct rent amount to be paid.

b. Deposit the check and send her an eviction notice.

    c. Deposit the check, reserving your legal rights to pursue eviction.

The incorrect answer, in most states, is "b," and both are "a" and "c" are correct. Once you accept and deposit a partial rent check without reserving your right to continue the eviction, you have accepted the tenant's payment again. If you want the remainder of the rent, you will have to start your eviction all over again.

You can deposit the rent check, as long as you reserve your rights to continue the eviction. This must be done on the rent check or money order, on the front or back of the check:

"For use and occupancy only. All legal rights still reserved to evict."

After you write this on the tenant's rent payment, make a copy for your tenant's file folder, and make a copy to mail to the tenant before you deposit the check. If you have a Section 8 tenant, send a copy to the leasing manager as well. Cover all your bases to let everyone know that any money you accept as partial rent does not mean you are not going to continue the eviction. If you accept cash (which I do not recommend), you must send a rent receipt to the tenant reserving your legal rights, with a copy of the receipt in the tenant file folder.

When you rented the apartment, it was for the use of your space. If you have multiple tenants, such as roommates, it does not matter which roommate did or did not pay a share of the rent. You rented the space. You want all of the rent each month.

*Note: There are 18 states that allow a tenant to terminate your notice to quit if the rent is paid in full three days before the end of the notice to quit term (**www.thelpa.com**).*

Rent Payment Agreement

One way to address a tenant's arrears is to allow the tenant to follow a rent repayment agreement (see Appendix). This is where the tenant pays the current rent plus an amount on the arrears every month until the rent is totally caught up.

Of course, if the tenant fails to pay according to the agreement or is unable to get government, family, or friend assistance, you must file for eviction. Do not stop an eviction just because you have a payment plan with the tenant or the state has promised you some money in arrears. You never know whether the tenant will be able to keep the agreement. It is also a good way to keep the flame to the tenant's feet. State budget cuts could prevent you from getting all or some of the money agreed to by the Department of Transitional Assistance. The tenant could have made the agreement in good faith, but the reality could become that he or she cannot keep it.

Do not stop an eviction while you are waiting for the tenant's income tax refund money to come in. This is a common way of stalling the eviction process. Most people commit their entire tax refund before they even get the check. Continue the eviction. If the tenant does give you his rent from his income tax refund check, consider yourself fortunate and deposit it immediately.

Apartment Exchange

As a landlord or property manager, it is incumbent on you to figure out creative ways to avoid an eviction for nonpayment of rent. An apartment exchange could be a way to prevent legal action.

You are entitled to raise the rent for your housing. At least every other year, you will need extra income to pay the increase in expenses. You also have some good tenants who have been with you for years. Are you ready to lose a good tenant because you raised the rent too high for them to pay? If you could find an apartment, or had one, that was less expensive for this person, would you make it available for your tenant to rent?

Sometimes, a homeowner thinks the only solution to a nonpayment of rent issue due to a rent increase is to evict the person or family. If you own more than one building, consider making a switch. For example, if your tenant is living in a three-bedroom apartment with just one child, ask if she would consider moving into a two-bedroom with a lower rent. You might have tenants who need a three-bedroom unit due to a family addition. If they like you as a landlord, and the apartments offered are in good condition and in a good neighborhood, they might rather go to another bedroom size than suffer the indignity and expense of being evicted.

If you discuss the rent increase with your tenant and find that it is too much for the family to pay, keep an open mind about finding alternatives to the eviction process. Fixing up two apartments, keeping good tenants, and getting the new rent you need from both apartments is sometimes cheaper than spending the funds to evict good tenants with nowhere else to go.

Allow Family Members to Move In

In a tight economy, making ends meet is difficult at best. You may experience, at some point, a request from your tenant to move in a family member or friend to help make ends meet with the rent. Some common-sense decisions must be made about your response.

Your primary reason for raising the rent is the need (or desire) for additional income. If you are paying all the utilities in each apartment, adding another tenant might defeat the purpose of the rent increase. But, no more than if the tenant has a baby or two.

On the other hand, a rent increase might cause your tenant to move out. This will create expenses, such as fixing up the apartment again, advertising for rental applicants, and processing rental applications to do credit checks, eviction checks, and other research on every applicant.

If you have a good, stable tenant and there is enough room in the apartment, allowing a family member or friend to move in to help pay the rent is not uncommon. If the tenant pays the utilities, there is no additional apartment cost, except wear and tear on the unit.

Make sure that you process a rental application and verify all of the new person's information, such as employment and credit report, before you allow the additional person to move in. If you do not, you might have kept your stable tenant, received more rent, and added a problem person to your apartment. Also, after you have verified that the new tenant is all right with you, either have both tenants sign a new lease or add the new tenant to the original lease as an addendum.

At the beginning of this chapter, I stated that these measures could stop the completion of an eviction, but they should never stop the beginning of an eviction. The eviction process should always continue while you and your tenant attempt to work things out to mutual satisfaction. It can always be stopped at any point, even after you have received the official notice of approval to move the tenant out of your place.

8 OTHER REASONS TO EVICT

Nonpayment of rent is not the only reason to evict a tenant. For those owners who use a lease, any violation of a clause or clauses in the lease is a reason to evict. If you do not have a lease, these are some destructive behaviors that merit the start of an eviction, especially if the tenant refuses to change the abusive behavior.

In cases other than nonpayment of rent, the need to be factual and detailed in whatever part of the lease is in violation is critical. One cannot say, for example, that you are evicting your tenant because he is a "drunk" or a "drug addict." Unless you are a professional in that field, you must address the behavior of the tenant, facts about actions, and not your personal opinion. What specific negative behavior does the tenant exhibit that causes you to want your apartment back?

FIRST, CONSIDER THE SOURCE

Before you go into eviction action, look into all the facts. Be aware that tenants or neighbors might not tell the truth when they complain. Who is making the complaint? What is their motive for complaining to you? To get your tenant evicted? So she can move into another apartment in your building? There are tenants who might covet another's apartment and will say or do anything to get that tenant evicted.

Do not take action that might be based on false accusations. When you evict a tenant with a family for cause, that tenant might have a hard time finding another apartment. The eviction case will be a public record for all other landlords and property managers to see and judge. Get proof before you start an eviction. If you cannot get proof, get it from legal authorities. If someone tells you your tenant is dealing drugs, talk to the local police captain before you confront the tenant. Talk to the tenant, let him or her know that a complaint has been lodged, and discuss it together.

There are still people who think that people of another ethnicity moving into their neighborhood will bring their property values down. If you have owned your property for a number of years with no problems, then rent to an ethic family, and all of a sudden you hear one complaint after another, consider the source. If the complaints are coming from a reliable source, like your next-door neighbor whom you have known for years, that should be a good source.

You have a responsibility to protect your investment and your tenants. Moving people in and out of your building because of false accusations will bankrupt you. Prevention of an eviction will save you money in the long run, if you do your homework. Consider the source, get your own evidence, or obtain written documentation from the local authorities.

HOARDERS

One reason to inspect your occupied apartments at least once a year is to review the condition of your property. You need to know how your tenant is treating your investment. You cannot afford to wait years until the tenant moves out before you know whether your tenant is abusive to the apartment. One reason for eviction is to seek the removal of a hoarding tenant.

Hoarding is a psychological condition. Hoarders save everything they possess or bring into their apartment. They create a severe fire hazard, collecting newspapers, magazines, old food containers, and the like, no matter how meaningless or what condition of the objects. Some hoarders will collect cats and dogs as well as materials.

Hoarding is a major dilemma. The tenant is psychologically helpless to throw anything away. Tenants are known to pile all their food, trash, and other useless materials from floor to ceiling. Hoarders can destroy a property with excessive clutter. It is much more than an eccentric life style. It is a fire waiting to happen. Their medical condition can have a negative impact on the entire building.

Hoarding tenants need help, medical as well as cleaning assistance, so much so, that unless the tenant gets medical help, the only solution is to evict the tenant. It is a public safety issue. The fire and building departments should be called to visit the apartment and help convince the tenant of the dangerous condition. If this is unsuccessful, call the housing department or city hall for some assistance.

Working with a hoarder is a lengthy process. It will not be solved in a month or two. You might feel sorry for the tenant. Still, you will have to decide to act on the greater issue of preserving your property and the safety of your other tenants. You might get your tenant to clear out the initial mess, but without extensive psychological help, the tenant will fill up the apartment again.

An eviction gives notice to the tenant and her friends or relatives that you are serious. Take pictures of the clutter for your day in court. Continue to work with the tenant and those trying to help him or her. But, even if the tenant is receiving medical help, continue the eviction.

EXTRA PEOPLE IN THE APARTMENT

You rented your two-bedroom apartment to a nice lady with a young son. One day, as you are visiting your property, you notice extra names on a tenant's mailbox and doorbell. You knock, and a strange man opens the door. You explain you are the landlord, and ask the man's identity. He informs you that he is your tenant's boyfriend. You ask the man to have your tenant call you when she arrives home.

When your tenant calls you, she does not deny that he is living with her. She explains that her boyfriend had his own apartment, but his roommate moved out. As he could not afford the rent, she allowed him to move in with her until he could find another place. Believe her story or not, she has still broken her lease.

Once you are aware that an extra person has moved into your building, you must address it immediately. It does not matter if the tenant pays all the utilities in the unit. It does not matter that you like either the new person or the tenant. It has to do with control. You have the right to control who lives in your building. That is why you have the clause that states a tenant must have written permission to add a person to his or her unit.

It might be for a legitimate reason. The tenant's father died and the mother moves in, or a niece comes from out of state and has nowhere else to live or cannot afford a place to live on her own. You might not even have a problem with it, but you are still entitled to have the tenant respect you as the building owner or manager. They should ask you if it is all right to move someone else in.

You have the right to approve everyone living in your building. If the tenant wants to move an extra person into your apartment, he or she must have your written consent. If you agree to review that request, the tenant must have that person complete a rental application, and you must confirm all the information. You still are not obligated to accept this person.

If you reject the extra person in the apartment, give the tenant a specific amount of time to vacate that person. If he or she continues to live there, you have the right to evict everyone in the apartment. The reason — an unauthorized person is occupying your apartment.

Excessive Noise

If you live in the same building with your tenant, you will be acutely aware of any problems with excessive noise. If you do not live in the same building with your tenants, you will receive complaints about the problem. Never devalue these complaints, because if not addressed, it could cause your rent-paying tenants to move out or your reputation as a good owner or manager to be damaged. Here are some indications that you have an excessive noise problem:

- Music so loud that it wakes you up when you are sleeping

- Loud music that continues for more than an hour

- Music so loud it can be heard outside of the tenant's apartment

- Music played loudly on the front porch

- Parties every other weekend, with large numbers of people dancing and thumping on the floor above you or your other tenants

- Music so loud that people outside in the street can hear it

- Loud music or other noise that begins before 7 a.m. or continues after 11 p.m.

- Constant thumping on the floor of the apartment over another tenant's unit that sounds like someone stomping on the floor or wrestling

What happens between tenants before they talk to you is what freelance writer and renter Sheila Webster-Heard[9] describes in her article, "Living in Harmony: Dealing with Dreadful Neighbors" (**www.ezinearticles.com**): "(But), if you're like a ton of us who has experienced the person who recognizes they are disturbing the peace and they really do not care, your best bet would be not to knock on their door, because it will enrage them. The music may play louder and longer, and you're going to be livid."

This is why you are contacted as the owner or manager of the building — to prevent confrontations between tenants. Like Webster-Heard explains, the tenant involved always seems to know who made the complaint. Maybe the complaining tenant tried to reason with him before talking to you. Some problem tenants are bold enough to go to the complaining tenant and try to intimidate him or her from complaining again. This is why you need to get involved and get the information you need to rectify the problem.

What if the tenant being complained about is considered one of your "good" tenants? Or, what if the tenant is a friend or relative of yours? Even if the tenant is paying top rent and is satisfactory to you in every other way, you must confront the tenant.

Clearly, if you are receiving the complaint from another tenant, there has been no mutual agreement about what is acceptable and what is not. Once the noise leaves the tenant's apartment, it is in your area of responsibility to rectify. If you do not take charge, you could find yourself without the complaining tenant, who might be exasperated by the ongoing noise and your lack of action and move out.

A tenant will break a lease because of excessive noise. No one would like it if every time he or she came home from work, exhausted and ready for a nap, had to hear someone else's music, never what he or she likes, blasted for more than an hour every other evening and on weekends.

It is time to intervene and talk to the tenant when you get the first complaint from other tenants in the building. You must establish authority over your tenants' right to the quiet enjoyment of their apartments. You cannot ask the two tenants to try to work things out. You need to be the mediator, or you are violating the tenants' rights to living in a peaceful environment. Below are some suggestions for getting control over the matter:

- Do not blame the tenant making the complaint. It is within his or her right to ask you to take control of the tenant abusing the other tenants on your property. Thank the tenant for providing you with the information.

- You need to get the complaining tenant to be specific about the problem. Ask that the times and dates of every disturbance be provided in writing or in an e-mail.

- To prevent the offending tenant from knowing who made the complaint, go to the building at the time the music most often happens.

- Knock on the door and speak with the tenant. Let him or her know that you were in the building and heard the loud music. Ask for cooperation in keeping the noise level down.

- Do not get into a discussion about whether the music is loud. If you can hear it in the public hallway, it is too loud, and you have the final say.

- Document the discussion as an incident report (see Appendix), and place it in the tenant's file.

ILLEGAL ACTIVITIES IN THE APARTMENT

I once inspected a building and found a long extension cord from a tenant's apartment to the public hallway outlet. Apparently, the tenant's electricity was cut off. He was using the hallway electricity. I pulled out the cord, knocked on the tenant's door, gave it to him, and requested he not do it again. I went back to my office and wrote up an incident report, made and mailed the appropriate copies, and placed the original in the tenant's file.

You can evict a tenant who smokes marijuana, if you can prove it. You smell marijuana coming from a tenant's apartment on a frequent basis. You do not consider yourself the police or drug enforcement unit (unless you are). You knock on the door, and when the tenant answers, the smoke fumes fly in your face. Explain that if you can smell it in the hallway, others can, too. Remind him he is using an illegal drug, and you do not want to have to evict him because of a hopefully casual habit. Go home and write an incident report in case you have to evict for cause.

Whether you choose to begin legal action, illegal activities must be brought to the tenant's attention. The incident report is to remind you of various conversations and actions you might have taken over a period of weeks or months. Do not depend on your memory. When you send a copy to your attorney, he can review it and let you know whether you should take additional action.

CONSTRUCTIVE EVICTION

You and your tenant have been in constant battle since the tenant moved in. Constant repair demands and late rent payments have made life so miserable for you that you want to get rid of the property. Instead, you decide that enough is enough. You refuse to make any repairs to the property anymore, especially the tenant's apartment, no matter how extensive the problem gets.

The tenant finds he is unable to get you to make repairs. The property is rendered uninhabitable as the building turns into an unsafe place to live. Ultimately, the tenant feels he or she has no other choice but to move out of your apartment. This is called a "constructive eviction" and is likely illegal. The tenant is forced to move out due directly to the homeowner's failure to upkeep the property or failure to take specific action to prevent disrepair.

Some examples of a constructive eviction include:

- Changing the lock on the front entry door, then "forgetting" to give the tenant a key. Or, being conveniently unavailable to the tenant looking for the new key.

- A landlord may peep out of his first floor apartment, open his apartment door, and stare at every visitor to the upstairs apartment. This might appear to be a security technique, but in reality, it is an intimidation action, geared toward making visitors hesitant about going to the building.

- A landlord may decide to not fix the offending tenant's hot water tank for more than a week.

Some landlords call this behavior "self-help." They feel so out of control about having a person living in their apartment without paying the rent that they end up doing things out of anger or frustration. The real intent of the homeowner is to get the tenant to move out of the apartment without going through the legal eviction process. It is an illegal and unprofessional way to handle a legal case.

The owner's strategy is to get the tenant to decide it is better to move out of the apartment than to endure the landlord's failure to be a responsible homeowner. Even if the tenant stops paying the rent, the landlord is willing to allow nonpayment if his or her neglectful actions force the tenant out of the building.

The repercussions of such slipshod actions can be extensive. If a tenant can prove that the failure of the landlord caused the tenant to move out under duress, fines and penalties can be assessed against the owner. In addition to penalties paid, whatever damages occurred to the tenant's belongings because of the owner's failure to take responsible action could be added.

There are times when constructive eviction does not apply. During an anticipated renovation of a property, residents must receive a specific amount of time to move out so rehabilitation can begin. This is different from occupying a property, expecting to continue occupation on an ongoing basis. The homeowner is responsible for providing the necessary environment for tenants to inhabit the property until everyone has moved out.

In one situation, a property could no longer be inhabited without a substantial renovation, and all tenants were notified. They were relocated to other buildings at the homeowner's expense. They were offered the chance to move back in once the property was completed.

Still, there were three tenant holdouts. The owner had done everything possible to get those residents to move out, including monetary offers and paid moving expenses. Thinking they could get a better deal, they continued to hold out for more benefits.

During a cold spell, the heating system broke down, and pipes broke throughout the building. Repairing the system and pipes was not an option. It needed to be replaced, and the property was scheduled to be in rehabilitation at the time. The residents called the Housing Inspection Department and claimed constructive eviction.

The city inspectors went through the building and agreed it was uninhabitable. The city housing department advised the tenants to take the owner's relocation offer and leave the building. When they refused, the city condemned the building, and the residents were left to their own devices to find another place to live.

EXCESSIVE VISITORS OR FOOT TRAFFIC

Visitors to your building can be a problem, if there are more than five visitors to the same apartment every day or even every hour. You have the right to evict a tenant who has so many visitors that it disrupts the quiet enjoyment of the property. Examples of this include the following.

- Five to ten visitors a day, almost every day of the week.

- The same people show up every single day, sometimes several times a day.

- People show up all times of day and night, ringing

doorbells and disturbing the other tenants trying to sleep.

- Your entry door locks are constantly broken by the visitors seeking entry into the building.

- The visitors loiter in and around the property. They do not stay in the tenant's apartment, nor do they leave the vicinity.

- People show up several times a day and stay less than 15 minutes to a half-hour, creating excessive foot traffic in the building.

All this traffic may signal heavy drug activity or even drug dealing. But, the owner does not have to prove drug dealing. He only has to verify and prove the amount of traffic and the excessive or negative behavior of the visitors to the property.

File an incident report showing when and how much traffic comes into the building, take a copy of this to the police department or drug enforcement unit, and bring your incident reports to the housing court judge.

PET LIABILITY

Why evict a tenant with a pet? A pet, dog, cat, hamster, bird, fish, rabbit, or other pet can provide months or years of happy companionship, contentment, pleasure, and for many people, a sense of family. A dog or cat can also wreak havoc in an apartment, vandalize it, emit a foul odor, mark its "territory" to the detriment of everyone's sense of smell, be excessively noisy, and can necessitate keeping its waste box clean on a regular basis.

A dangerous pet has the capacity to bite, maul, or seriously injure others.

Unfortunately, there are tenants who have not done their best to maintain their pet's cleanliness in an apartment. Think of fleas, multiple litters of young, and birdseed in carpet, as well as mating noise, for example. For these reasons, many landlords do not allow pets in their apartments. They do not want to have to clean up behind a tenant's pet mess, during or after the tenancy. In many states, you cannot collect an extra fee for a pet deposit. You have to use the security deposit to restore your vacancy caused by pet and tenant damage.[10]

There are other reasons why pets are not allowed in apartments. Some tenants want to have and keep pets that are considered violent, dangerous, and unfriendly to people. There are pets associated with brutality, severe mauling, and even death by biting, beating, and tearing of human or other animal skin. These days, the pets that are considered the most dangerous are pit bull and Rottweiler dogs. Doberman pinschers, Akitas, and the like have all been frequently referred to as "attack dogs."

Tenants enjoy having these pets for security, but some do not always control their pet's behavior or will not keep the pet appropriately leashed. Some tenants will not even keep their dog or cat in their apartment, allowing it to wander around the public hallways all day until they get home.

States do have animal liability laws, and you should look up the laws for your state. Liability usually refers to the owner of the pet. For example, if the owner of a German shepherd allows the dog to wander the streets without a leash and someone gets bitten, the dog's owner is liable for the damages, pain, and suffering to the person involved.

As a homeowner, you too could have an insurance liability if you know you have a tenant with a violent or dangerous dog, especially if the tenant is not allowed a pet in the lease. If you have this information, and you do nothing to get the tenant to keep it leashed or to remove it, you could also be sued if the dog bites another of your tenants or a visitor to the building.

Your failure to take action against a tenant with a vicious animal could open you up to a potential lawsuit. If a dog were to injure another tenant in the building, you would be on the receiving end of the lawsuit, as the one with the deepest pocket. In this regard, filing eviction action against a tenant who refuses to give up his beloved pit bull could be the best approach to take.

Similarly, by not inspecting your apartment at least on an annual basis, you would not discover that your tenant had more than a dozen cats or dogs in the apartment. There have been countless news stories on tenants who collect animals, only to have the situation run out of control. By the time the landlord finds out about the pet collection, the police, animal rights activists, the news media, and the court system have gotten involved.

The potential damage to your apartment from weeks or months of animal feces, open food, vermin and insects, and cats and dogs allowed to run unabated could run into thousands of dollars and a nightmare for you and your homeowner's insurance company. Inspect your apartment at least once a year to avoid a potentially nasty eviction due to uncontrolled pets.

Begin to control the pet situation and start a potential eviction case by reminding the tenant in writing that he or she does not have your written approval to have a pet. Give the tenant a reasonable amount of time to get rid of the pet(s). If the pet is still on the property, the second letter should inform the tenant that the next correspondence you send will be an eviction notice. Send a copy of this letter to your attorney and your homeowner's insurance company.

You should also record and file complaints about the animal(s) from other tenants, and record your own observations as part of your evidence for court. If you can get a picture of your tenant walking the dog outside, that is good evidence.

Bottom line: either you run the property, or your tenant will. If you have a lease that says no pets, you have to abide by it, even if the tenant is one of your best. All you need is a tenant to fall down urine-soaked hallway stairs, or a visitor to the property to get bitten by your tenant's "friendly" pit bull allowed to run unabated in the hallway, to be sued. Even if the tenant is on Section 8, and HUD is paying the bulk of the rent, the time and expense involved in fighting a lawsuit, which goes for months, will cost you far more than the Section 8 rent paid to you each month.

ASSISTIVE ANIMALS

A homeowner and a property manager need to understand and differentiate between a pet and an assistive animal. An assistive animal is not a pet. These are special animals (sometimes called service animals), whose sole purpose is to help the tenant live and get around from place to place independently. A seeing-eye dog is an assistive animal.

There are also assistive animals, such as monkeys and cats, as well as dogs, that live with a tenant for emotional stability, or to assist the tenant in getting dressed. Federal law mandates that these types of animals are not considered or treated as a pet but as a tool. Disabled people who own these animals have been given meticulous training on how to care for their assistant. The dog, monkey, or other animal has also received comprehensive training on how to care for its owner, as well as how to behave in public and when others are around the house.

The tenant can provide you with written documentation on the service animal. It will come from either a doctor or the organization that provides the animal.

OTHER NON-PETS

Farm animals, like chickens, pigs, or goats, should not be considered pets in an urban city. These animals are associated with food products. Some tenants keep these types of animals to kill for a special ceremony or event. Meanwhile, they live in your apartment or basement until the day they are needed to feed guests.

There are pets that are also endangered species or are considered wildlife. There are state laws that determine whether a person is holding a pet, endangered species, or farm animal in a city dwelling illegally. Contact your city or state animal control department for specific information if you believe your tenant has an illegal pet or animal in the apartment.

After seeing many news programs where endangered species and jungle animals are held in apartments, my first action as a homeowner would be to call the police first to get the animal off the property, then start eviction action to get the tenant off the property. If you know that your tenant is keeping an exotic animal in his or her apartment and you do nothing about it, you could be liable if it should get out of the apartment, run amuck in the building, or bite someone.

Some tenants will remove the animal rather than be evicted. Other tenants would rather be evicted than get rid of their pet. You will need to prove that the pet lives in the apartment. Good ways to prove the pet lives with the tenant are:

- Schedule an apartment inspection after giving 24 to 48 hours notice to see if there is evidence of a pet.

- See pet food in the tenant's trash bags.

- See kitty litter in the tenant's trash bags.

- See a kitty litter box in the back hallway in front of the tenant's apartment door.

- Take a picture of the tenant walking his or dog in front of the building or coming in or out of the house.

- Take a picture of the children playing with their pet in front of the house.

- Visit the tenant — the dog or cat may come to the door with the tenant.

- Bring witnesses or notarized written testimonies saying they have seen the pet(s) and when.

- Look for birdseed on the floor when you do your apartment inspection.

- Look for bird feces and/or feathers on curtains at the top of the windows and take a picture (with a newspaper showing the date of the inspection).

EXCESSIVE USE OR DAMAGE TO THE UNIT

You have the right to evict a tenant who is laying waste to and deteriorating the condition of your apartment. When you moved the tenant in, you should have completed an apartment inspection or condition report (see Appendix). This is a standard form that shows the condition of the apartment when the tenant moved in. Ten days after the tenant moved in, you should have asked whether there were any repairs that you forgot to complete. This should be written down and repaired immediately and the results added to your tenant's file.

Once the apartment has been inspected and all outstanding repairs have been completed and recorded, any needed repairs during the tenancy should be for wear and tear only. Wear and tear is a series of repairs that are needed solely because of normal use of an apartment over an extended amount of time.

A repair outside of normal wear and tear would be if you provided window shades, and six months later, they are all torn up; this is not necessarily excessive damage, especially if the tenant has children. If, however, you need to replace those window shades every three months, this is not normal wear and tear.

If you put down a new carpet, and six months later, it has dark spots, cigarette burns, and enough dirt to plant crops, this is excessive damage. When the tenant moves out, it is better to have an outside cleaning company try to deal with the carpet. This way, if the company cannot get out the spots or clean it to your satisfaction, the cleaning company can put this in writing as evidence of tenant damage. The cost of the cleaning company can be deducted from the security deposit.

One way to avoid taking eviction action is to inform the tenant in the lease that replacement shades are the tenant's responsibility after you provide the first set. The tenant might take better care of the shades, and you will not have to spend money replacing them or evicting the tenant.

When making repairs to the apartment costs you more than the rent you receive, it is time to ask the tenant to leave, especially if the tenant refuses to reimburse your costs for the repairs after you have given him or her a bill. Do not allow a tenant to lay waste to your unit repeatedly.

Excessive water consumption is a big concern for a landlord. According to the American Water Works Association, the average United States resident uses about 110 gallons a day. We use the most for toilets, followed by bathing, laundry and dishes, and cooking and drinking. In addition, a washing machine that is not properly installed can cause damage to the water pipes. Overflow from an unattended machine can damage the floor and ceiling of the apartment below. If you did not give permission for your tenant to have a washing machine and the tenant refuses to give it up, this could constitute grounds for excessive utility use and/ or damage caused by such use.

The same excessive use applies in other areas. If your tenant opens up a home-based beauty salon without your knowledge or permission, an increase in water consumption, not to mention foot traffic to your building, will happen. You have the right to ask the tenant to stop doing hair in the apartment or face eviction.

FIRE, HEALTH, AND SAFETY ISSUES

A homeowner or property manager needs to deal directly and firmly with tenants who do things that will put their lives and your building in jeopardy. Some examples of behaviors that must be corrected are:

- Tenants who remove safety devices from the apartment.

- Tenants who remove the batteries from smoke detectors so they will not go off when cooking.

- Tenants who remove the small fire extinguisher from the apartment kitchen.

- Tenants who remove the exhaust fan from the kitchen hood and do not replace it.

- Tenants who install illegal window bars on the first-floor apartment windows. Window bars are supposed to be the type that have a push bar, so that in the event of a fire, a person can push open the window bars to get out.

- Tenants who remove the window screens or cut them open to put in an air conditioner. This is damage to your apartment.

- Tenants who install a double-keyed lock on the apartment door. This is a lock where you have to use a key to get in or out of the apartment. Even though people will leave the key in the inside lock, this is a dangerous type of lock. In a fire with smoke, people excited by the moment will sometimes jiggle the key out of the lock in the heat of the situation. In some states, it is illegal to install a double-keyed lock on an apartment door or entry doors.

- Tenants who smoke in bed and have set several small fires in the apartment. Each time the smoke detector avoided a disaster. The three-year tenant always pays promptly for whatever damage is caused. One day, he will not be so lucky. He needs to go.

- Tenants who are or become hoarders. This is a serious fire concern for the homeowner.

- Tenants who continually store garbage and trash in the back hallway on the floor and forget to put it out on the sidewalk or who will not use the trash cans or Dumpster provided for the building but leave bags next to them. Ironically, this is often the same tenant who will complain about mice and bugs.

In the case of a double-keyed lock, get a letter from the fire marshal's office or copy a quote from the state sanitary or building code, and send it to the tenant. Then, give the tenant three to five days to remove the lock and put a proper and legal lock on the apartment door. Go back and see whether the tenant complied.

If the tenant still has the double-keyed lock installed, notify the fire department or housing department in writing as an official complaint against the tenant. At the same time, notify the tenant that in the next three to five days, you will remove the lock and change it to the legal version, keyed to the building master key system. Put a copy of the letter of notification in the tenant's file folder as proof.

If you have a management company, this is its job. Have it provide you with written proof that the property manager has dealt with the problem and that the unit is now in compliance with the law. Here are more problems you need to quickly address:

- The tenant fails to put out the trash every week, and weeks of garbage collects in the apartment.

- The tenant starts to run an illegal day care center from the apartment.

- The tenant is repairing cars in your driveway or parking lot.

- A home business has many extension cords around the apartment that could be a fire hazard.

- The tenant fails to notify you that there are mice, roaches, water bugs, or other vermin infesting the apartment. By the time you find out, the problem is huge.

Tenants have a responsibility to use preventive ways to avoid having an infestation and to report vermin and insect problems to the owner or management when they exist. Failure to do so could be a reason to take legal action to get back control of your apartment.

ADDITIONAL PEOPLE MOVE IN

It is not your business if your tenant has a boyfriend or girlfriend, friend or relative that visits the apartment. If the tenant has visitors over for a vacation, for example, two weeks is a reasonable time for the live-in visit. Everyone has the right to have company come over.

It becomes your business if your tenant moves one or more family members or friend(s) into the apartment. Again, one must be reasonable and practical. If the additional person is a new baby, an adoption, or the tenant's mother must move in to be assisted by her son or daughter, consideration should be made.

On the other hand, if an additional person or people will cause the apartment to be illegally overcrowded, something must be said and/or done. A lease that outlines how and when additional people may live at the apartment should address this situation in advance.

YOUR OTHER TENANTS THREATEN TO MOVE OUT

Bad tenants like to boast about getting over on the landlord or property manager. If you lose your eviction case, the tenant will brag even louder. The behavior will become worse, because the tenant now thinks she got away with something. You have to start your case over again. Meanwhile, the tenant still occupies the apartment rent-free (if she was being evicted for nonpayment).

Do not expect your other tenants to put up with some or even one of the above lease violations from their neighbors. They pay their rent too, on time and every month. Tenants sometimes talk to each other, especially about a bad tenant. Your rent-paying tenants will not appreciate you allowing another tenant to get away with not paying.

Also, there are tenants who will leave a building because of your failure to act on the lease violations of another tenant. If they are kept awake every morning by their neighbor's radio and you do nothing about it, they will find somewhere else to live.

Once you file your eviction papers, it is a matter of public record. Inform your tenant in private that you are taking legal action.

INTOLERABLE APARTMENT RENOVATIONS

Most reasonable landlords will allow a tenant, especially a long-term one, to make some moderate changes to the apartment. Things that will not change the structure of a unit and will make living in the apartment feel more like home are allowed. I have, for example, allowed a tenant to remove wall paneling and paint the walls a pastel color for his personal visual comfort. He did a good job, and he was happier with his bedroom.

When a tenant makes a change to your apartment that is clearly harmful to the unit, action must be taken to reclaim your investment space. These are some real examples of apartment renovations I have had to address with legal action:

- Painting the entire apartment with fluorescent art

- Painting the entire apartment, walls and ceilings, in black or dark brown

- While painting the apartment, the tenant accidentally drops paint all over the living room carpet

- Changes that will cost more than the security deposit to return the unit to its former condition

When you ask the tenant to pay to return the apartment to its previous status and the tenant refuses, go to eviction court.

PHYSICAL CONFRONTATIONS

Physical confrontations are situations that should signal that it is time for your relationship with your tenant to end. These are cases that have been seen and heard in housing court:

- Your tenant controls the heat in your two-family house. You live upstairs. You go downstairs to ask your tenant to turn the heat down. Agitated, the tenant hits you in the head with a 2-by-4 board, then drags you unconscious out of the hallway into the snow on the front porch.

- The tenant beats you up or the two of you get into a fistfight when you complain about his or her children making too much noise at night.

- Your tenant likes to "visit" his neighbors whenever he or she has had too much to drink. He/she knocks on the door until a neighbor opens it. Then he talks and talks to the tenant, about nothing in particular, becoming a pest. He also, on occasion, will throw up in the hallway on his way up the stairs to his apartment. This happens at least two times a week.

It would be difficult to put a person out on the streets just because you did not like him. In most states, you need a valid reason to evict a tenant from your apartment. There must be some violation or "cause" to evict a tenant. You just cannot knock on the tenant's door and announce, "I want you out of here by next month!" In every case, you must send a written, formal, legal notice to the tenant to vacate the premises.

If your tenant assaults you, call the police to register a formal complaint and get a police report. If you need to file a restraining order against your tenant, you need to follow through with an eviction notice. You have a right not to be intimidated or fearful of an aggressive or physically abusive tenant.

EVICTING A FRIEND OR RELATIVE

The eviction of a friend or relative has to be one of the most difficult lawsuits, if not the most emotionally draining, of all types of evictions. You might be one of the lucky ones who can rent to a friend or relative with no side effects, but one day, there might come a time when you have to look your friend or family member in the eyes and ask him or her to leave your apartment.

In the eviction of a relative stranger, even a long-term tenant, the process is not personal, just business. The tenant cannot pay the rent; thus, he has to leave. It is the end of an association with minimal emotional ties between the tenant and the landlord.

The eviction of a friend or relative is one in which sides may be chosen. Once the eviction notice has been delivered, do not expect many friends or allies to come to your aid. Depending upon the circumstances of the eviction, you can expect to have your life made miserable by anyone affected by your decision.

This is because the expectations of a friend or relation are much higher than that of a stranger. If there is a tenancy problem, the expectation is that you will treat the tenant more as a friend or relative than as a financial investment problem. You will be asked to accept less than you normally would for rent arrears, to wait longer for your rent, and to accept behaviors that you would not normally tolerate.

For example, let us say you need to raise the rent. A rent increase could be perceived as a betrayal of your friendship. Your aunt could think you are taking advantage of her. It does not make sense, but when money is concerned, all bets are off. As far as a friend or relative is concerned, you are in his or her pocket. A belief that you are soaking your tenant for more money that you "really need" could cause your family member to not pay the increase.

Be clear and resolved about why the eviction must take place. Have all your written documentation in place. Check all your paperwork, rent cards, letters of warning, and other documentation before you send your notice to quit. Make sure you have a solid case before starting the eviction. Conduct a due diligence of your property and the legal case.

Hard feelings will sometimes come with the rental and eviction territory. Do not expect to be able to discuss the case calmly with the offended tenant, and do not expect a cool head to prevail over your eviction action. If you evict your nephew, expect your sister or brother to be angry with you. Your friend might think you are a jerk for evicting her because she parties loudly every weekend, disturbing your other tenants. Your aunt may not come to your aid when your niece does not pay the rent.

When a blood relative is evicting another blood relative, blood could be shed before the battle is over. Few people want to be in the middle of a turf war. You might find yourself isolated and alone during the eviction process until everything has settled. This is why most landlords refuse to rent to a friend or family member. It is preferred to have only one relationship than to confuse the personal relationship by adding a legal one.

Having everyone go through an application process, regardless of their status with you, establishes the ground rules from day one. Without it, the tenant could feel that he or she was taken in as a friend and then treated otherwise when things got tough. It helps to set up the lines of separation between the friendship and the tenancy.

Below are some tips for evicting a friend or relative:

Do not take shortcuts during the legal process. Do everything strictly by the book. A wounded friend or relative who knows your personal business becomes a worthy adversary in a legal case. He or she will use whatever information is available to fight you.

The jury is still out as to whether you should serve the initial notice of lease termination personally or use a constable. The friend or family member will find the sting of legal action just as shocking, no matter how the news is given. Keep your distance and have everything done by a third party.

Exercise the same professional manner in dealing with the loved one as you would with a stranger. Try to keep your emotions out of the situation. Avoid discussing the case at length with your now adversarial tenant. The less said, the less information that can be used against you in court.

Refuse to discuss your eviction case with friends and relatives. Your tenant friend or relative deserves the same amount of privacy and dignity as your other tenants. If your friends and/or relatives want to speak with you to "mediate" the situation, let them know that it is a private matter and you cannot discuss the case.

Put any rent arrears payment plans in writing. Continue the eviction case, and present the payment plan to the judge. Have the judge enter the payment plan in the court decision. Then, if the plan is broken, it is broken with the court, not you. Your friend or relative will be less likely to violate a court agreement.

Some landlords hire an attorney to process their eviction cases specifically against a friend or relative. When your friend or relative calls you about the eviction notice, refer all comments and questions to the attorney. Resist the temptation to explain why you started the action. With an attorney, you are taken out of the middle position. Let the lawyer earn the fee by listening to the anger, frustration, and feelings of betrayal of the friend or relative.

If you need to take legal action against a friend or relative who is your tenant, do it. Do not be intimidated by the personal association with you. Your real estate is a business investment. If you remember this during the process, you will be able to separate the two relationships.

No one wants to be evicted, especially by a person who is considered a pal and confidant. The bitter taste of humiliation, feeling of betrayal, and anger will remain long after the actual legal action. Before renting your vacant apartment out again, remember the experience. Decide whether the rent is worth the possible loss of friendship or the family discord.

> *Leon (fictional name) rented his second-floor apartment to his sister-in-law Sarah more than 20 years ago. At the time, she was new to the city, and he had just purchased his first three-family home with his wife, Michelle, and family. Over the years, things were fine between tenant and in-law Sarah upstairs and landlord and in-law Leon downstairs. There was a sense of comfort, family, and security over the years. Sarah paid the rent on time each month, and Leon liked having a close relative live on the property.*

> *One day, Leon realized that he needed to raise the rent on his sister-in-law's two-bedroom apartment. Real estate taxes, the water bill, and the heat and hot water, which he paid for, were high. He needed more income from the house. After agonizing over how much he should charge, he decided on a $50 per month increase. He thought that amount was fair, particularly as the last time he had raised the rent on her unit was seven years ago.*

His wife and adult children thought he was being overly generous. They wanted him to charge more for the two-bedroom apartment. The fair market rent in the neighborhood was well above what Sarah was currently paying, even with the $50 increase. Leon was a good landlord. It was nothing personal.

Sarah had a good career and the benefit of seven years without a rent increase. Leon painted her apartment on schedule every three years and kept her unit maintained. The rent increase would not be a strain for her to pay.

On the other hand, Leon had been absorbing the increased expenses for years. Sarah had been a good tenant, and the mortgage was paid off years ago. Leon knew he required an increase. In fact, he had needed to raise the rent a few years ago, but he did not want to appear greedy.

When Sarah received the 30-day rent increase letter, she felt betrayed. She was incensed that he wrote her a letter instead of telling her in person. She felt the amount was too high, given the small size of the second bedroom. A few days later, Sarah gave Leon a long list of repairs that she wanted done before she would pay the increase.

Leon's wife Michelle took the side of her husband. She could not understand why her sister was being so unreasonable over $50 a month. The fact that Sarah had given them a list of repairs, when Leon painted *her apartment every three years for 20 years and had repaired whatever Sarah had asked for in the past, made Michelle angry.*

Sarah informed Leon that she would not pay the rent increase until every repair she indicated was done to her satisfaction. Leon did not pursue eviction. The repairs were all made as requested. He preferred to keep the peace in the family house.

Sarah never paid the rent increase. By the time all the repairs were completed, Sarah had found another apartment. She rented a one-bedroom apartment across town. Her rent was more than three times what she was paying at Leon's house, and she had to pay her own utilities. The incident left a tension between them for years afterward. Leon refused to rent to family members again.

Although an eviction never happened in this case, you can see how bad it could have been. When renting to a friend or relative, think the worse-case scenario if you have to evict that person. You know their personality and temperament. Imagine how low that person is willing to go to humiliate or retaliate against you if you begin an eviction lawsuit.

For every case like the one above, there are positive stories to tell. There are many good tenant-relative stories in the property management industry. But it is far better to have a good friend or relative than an ugly eviction where your family business is heard in open court.

DO NOT MIX BUSINESS WITH PLEASURE

One should always keep one's personal and business lives apart. Certainly in the real estate management business, I subscribe to that theory. I have seen the two conflict too many times.

Shania (fictional name) was the property manager of a small mom-and-pop company. A husband-and-wife team owned several residential, multi-family properties. Shania enjoyed working at the company and knew that her bosses appreciated her work.

One day, it became clear to Shania that the husband was having more than a work relationship with a tenant. She knew this because when she went to visit the tenant to collect the rent, the tenant told her so. The tenant also advised Shania to get the rent directly from her boss.

Shania was uncertain what to do next. A few days later the wife, obviously suspecting something, insisted that Shania go back to the attractive tenant and collect the rent. The tenant again insisted that she get the rent from the husband. When Shania approached the husband, he feigned ignorance of the relationship. Shania felt caught in the middle of a dilemma.

One day the wife, blaming the property manager for not being diligent enough in collecting the rent from the tenant, criticized Shania. Shania decided to take action. She went to the husband and told him that she was tired of being in the middle of a personal situation and that she intended to do her job. She would begin eviction proceedings against the tenant, and she expected him to run interference with his wife and the tenant.

Soon after she filed the nonpayment of rent eviction notice on the tenant/lover, the tenant paid her rent in full. She stayed current from that day on. Shania never found out who paid the rent, neither did she care. Her rent collection efforts did the job.

Homeowners have an obligation not to get their employees involved in their personal business. It is hard enough trying to manage the property. Owners should know better than to mix their business with personal lives. The rent and/or the tenancy, if not your company operations, will invariably suffer. And, you could lose a valuable employee who is unwilling to be caught in the middle.

9

SECTION 8 EVICTION

The Section 8 program is a federal housing program where the government subsidizes an amount of housing at fair market rent for each county in every state. In each county, the fair market rent the government is willing to pay per bedroom size is posted at **www.hud.gov**. If a landlord or property manager accepts the Section 8 program in a property, he or she must also accept the maximum rent the government is willing to pay.

A potential renter must apply for Section 8 and must meet specific income and other guidelines. If eligible and accepted to the program, the tenant pays 30 percent of the adjusted income for rent, and the landlord gets the remaining amount from the government each month.

The administrator of the Section 8 Program is the local public housing authority. When you rent to a tenant with a Section 8 certificate or voucher, you are, in effect, renting to two tenants — the tenant and the federal government. The local public housing authority represents the federal government in managing the Section 8 certificates and vouchers for the city where your apartment is located.

The Section 8 Program is voluntary in every state except

Massachusetts and New Jersey. Those states consider Section 8 funds from the federal government the same as income. Refusing to accept a Section 8 voucher or certificate for rent in those states is considered discrimination on the basis of the source of income.

When you evict the Section 8 tenant by sending him or her a notice to quit, you must serve the local housing authority at the same time. The leasing officer needs to receive a copy of everything you send the tenant. That includes all letters, notices, summonses, special apartment inspections, and any other relevant documents. Send it to the Section 8 leasing manager who processed the lease with you.

The same goes when reserving your legal rights to receive funds from the Section 8 administrator. You must notify the leasing officer that the Section 8 check received is for use and occupancy only, not rent. Failure to reserve your legal rights to evict on both the tenant's check and the Section 8 check could re-establish the tenancy, and you will have to start the eviction process over again.

Review your Section 8 lease and Housing Assistance Payment (HAP) Contract. It will give you instructions on your obligations as a Section 8 landlord regarding an eviction. The lease also tells you how you must conduct the eviction of one of its tenants. Follow the Section 8 lease procedures for eviction to the letter.

If you process an eviction without ever letting the Section 8 leasing department know what is going on, you may be stopped at any point by the Section 8 department. Do not forget this important part of your eviction suit.

To avoid starting a new tenancy, write, "For use and occupancy only. All legal rights reserved," on the back of both checks. Then make a copy of the front and back of the checks for the tenant's file. When you go to court and you are asked to prove that you reserved your rights every month during the eviction, you will have your evidence. Some states do not allow you to accept any money once you begin an eviction. Review your state eviction laws.

You could save yourself a good deal of time, trouble, and money by contacting your tenant's leasing officer and informing him or her of your problems before taking any legal action. The leasing officer is happy to assist you, especially if it will avoid an eviction.

EVICTION TIP

If a tenant is evicted for the use or sale of illegal drugs, that tenant could lose the Section 8 certificate or voucher permanently.

CODE VIOLATIONS WILL COST YOU MONEY

Before a Section 8 tenant can occupy your apartment, it and the building must pass an inspection. The Section 8 housing inspector will go through your building and pass or fail your unit. If it fails, you will be given an amount of time to correct the deficiencies. Once you make the corrections, call the Section 8 inspector and ask for a return inspection. Until you receive a full pass inspection from the Section 8 program, you cannot move in your tenant.

These inspections are in addition to any local vacancy inspection laws in your state. The Section 8 inspector may require you to complete one set of repairs. The local housing inspector may require you to complete another set of repairs. Believe it or not, both inspectors use the state sanitary or housing code from your state.

This is a good thing. If you ever have cause to evict a Section 8 tenant for excessive damage to the apartment, you will have two inspections that will show the unit and building were in good shape before he or she received the keys. Landlords often fail to bring the original Section 8 approved apartment inspection to court. This is a mistake, because it can help you win your damage eviction case.

This is one area where a Section 8 code violation will cost you money. Every day you are unable to rent your vacant apartment because of code violations costs you a daily rental vacancy loss (and a tax deduction). Another good thing — the tenant must pay the landlord the full security deposit, not just his or her 30 percent of income, before move-in.

The program can also cost you money after the tenant has moved into your unit. The Section 8 tenant has the right to call her leasing officer and ask for a Section 8 inspection to prove the lack of repairs. This is done to counter your nonpayment of rent case. If the Section 8 inspector finds repair issues, he or she will give you time to make the repairs. If not made in the amount of time the inspector requires, your Section 8 rent payments will stop.

Now, not only are you not getting the tenant's rent, you are not getting the Section 8 rent either, and you have to spend money to make the repairs. You can deduct all damages and unpaid rent from the tenant's security deposit, and you might be able to defray some of the damage repairs by sending an invoice to the leasing agent. However, the Section 8 Program might not approve rent and damages over and above the security deposit. You might have to go to small-claims court after reporting the unpaid rent and expenses to the three credit bureaus.

DO NOT DEPEND ON SECTION 8 TO HELP YOU IN COURT

In many states, the maximum rent Section 8 allows can be more than neighborhood rents. But there are also states where the government fair market rent can be as much as $300 a month more than the local market. There are some landlords who decide not to evict a rent-delinquent tenant on Section 8, and here is why.

The two-bedroom, fair market rent in 2007 in Los Angeles was $1,485 a month. Let us say the tenant pays 30 percent of her income, or $125 per month, for rent. The landlord therefore collects $1,360 from Section 8. Some landlords would rather go along and collect the $1,360 per month from Section 8 than go to the expense of eviction court for $125.

When you do not begin nonpayment of rent legal action, you send the message that what share the tenant pays does not matter, as long as you are still getting the bulk of the rent. Ironically, the less rent a tenant has to pay, the more likely the rent will be late every month or not paid at all. If the amount of the rent is small, the tenant thinks she can easily get "caught up."

There are some judges who do not want to be bothered with 119 a $125 nonpayment of rent eviction case. They hear hundreds of cases much worse than one month's rent less than $200. Do not let the judge intimidate you. You are within your rights to file your case. One tenant not paying his rent will spread to any other tenants who find out about it.

Your $125 eviction case is just as important as those property managers and public housing authorities in court with hundreds of tenant cases owing more than $2,500 each for nonpayment of rent. Remind the judge you are a one-property or small rental income owner and cannot afford to lose any money to pay the mortgage. Go to mediation if asked, but stay firm that you are not looking for a continuance but a judgment in your favor.

CHAPTER

10 EVICTING TENANTS WITH SPECIAL CIRCUMSTANCES

Not every eviction is the same. Each eviction case should be approached on its own merits. Some cases need to be handled with a certain level of sensitivity. Other evictions should be coldly calculated to ensure the problem will never darken your door again. The success of an eviction depends on the personality of the tenant and landlord. It depends on who wants what more than the other. It requires meticulous detail and a sense of urgency, organization, and follow-through.

Before embarking on any eviction case, it is your responsibility to know the eviction laws of your state. Visit your statehouse bookstore or do an Internet search for evictions in your state for information. Tenants have a wealth of agencies and associations to help them fight you. You need to collect and read whatever information is available to fight back.

DRUG EVICTIONS

A drug-related eviction has the potential to be one of the most costly legal actions to take against a tenant. These days, illegal drug use has been expanded to mean much more than marijuana or cocaine. Illegal drugs can include prescription drugs, methamphetamine, crack cocaine, heroin, and oxycodone.

Regardless of what drug is involved, your property is in jeopardy every day you have illegal drugs or drug use on your property.

You could have an excellent, rent-paying tenant one month, and a drug using, non-rent-paying, destructive tenant the next. A current user of illegal drugs is not part of a protected class. An active drug user is not covered under the federal program, the Americans with Disabilities Act of 1990. Tenants who participate in a supervised rehabilitation program and are no longer engaged in the use of illegal drugs are covered under this Act.

Here are examples of what can happen to a property with illegal drugs in it:

- Drugs will chase away your good tenants, who will move out in fear or frustration.

- The value of your property, and perhaps even the neighboring properties, decreases.

- You could lose as much as three months' rent while you are fighting the eviction and more after the tenant moves out and you find extensive damage to the unit.

- Some drugs are so volatile, such as crack cocaine and methamphetamine, that improper use could set your house on fire.

Do not let your good feelings about a tenant interfere with your duty as a property owner. Do not cross your fingers, hoping it will stop. Your tenant will only get worse, your rent will not be paid, and the tenant will lie to you about everything.

Drug dealers consider what they do as their business. Drug dealers will pay their rent on time every month. Some drug dealers will move in with a good tenant, take over the apartment, and ruin the tenant's chance of being able to keep the apartment. When this happens, you cannot separate the two of them. Everyone in the apartment must be evicted.

HOW TO GET RID OF THE PROBLEM

See the problem for yourself. You cannot always depend on your a complaining tenant's interpretation of what he or she sees. If there is drug use, you will not have to wait long in your car before you see a pattern. Take pictures and notes of your observations by date, time, and number of people going in and out of the apartment. Take your notes and pictures to the police, preferably the drug enforcement unit. See Chapter 5 for additional information.

Put up "no trespassing" or "no loitering" signs. The police will need those signs on the top of the outside door for permission to enter your property, or to ask loiterers to move on. If you feel these types of signs have a negative connotation against your property, you can always take them down after the tenant is gone.

You should talk to the tenant about your concerns based on your observations. Never accuse the tenant of dealing or using drugs. You can ask, but the tenant is not going to confirm your suspicions. It might even start an argument. Even if you think you have proof, do not divulge this information to the tenant. Why let him or her know your game plan?

Do not involve your other tenants in the building other than to write up an incident report whenever they call to complain. Let them know you will do something about the problem. It would not be good to discuss your plans for addressing the problem. You never know whether other tenants are in on the situation.

Do not use your other tenants as witnesses against your illegal drug tenant, because whether you win or lose the eviction, those tenants might be retaliated against. There have been serious repercussions on tenants or neighbors who provided information on criminal activities and those involved. Unless he or she volunteers and knows the possible ramifications of his or her actions, do not ask for help making your drug eviction case.

Go to Chapter 5 for more information on how your local Drug Enforcement Unit can help.

Evicting the Tenant Handyman or Live-In Manager

You may decide to keep up your property on your own. Perhaps you know a few things about maintaining heating systems, carpentry, and how to paint and plaster. You figure you have only three apartments to care for, that you live in one of them, and you can handle it.

Depending on the number of units under ownership, forty-five percent of all multifamily homeowners spend from one to eight hours a week devoted to the maintenance and management of their property. This is according to the 2004 U.S. Census Bureau's Property Owners and Managers Survey, Housing and Household Economic Statistics Division (46.4% of owners with less than 5 units; 39.9% with 5 to 49 units; 20.5% of homeowners with 50 or more units). Other homeowners either do not have the time or the experience necessary to put toward their property.

As you are getting a good profit from the property, you thought it would be beneficial if you could get someone who lives in your building to clean and do repairs. The tenant would be compensated by a small reduction in the rent. This way, you have someone who is always on the property and can clean, shovel, mow, and take care of whatever repairs are needed.

Unfortunately, your live-in handyman might not be what you expected. As a tenant, he was good, and he appreciated the cut in rent. But, after a few months, working his own full-time job and taking care of the building proved to be too much for him. Alternatively, you might decide there is not enough work to be done at the property to justify the amount of rent that is deducted each month. You let him know that he will no longer be your handyman and give him notice of his termination and a 30-day notice that he will have to pay the full rent on his unit.

If you were cutting $100 a month from his rent to care for the building, he might not be able to cover the full rent again. He has been living on a different budget, and cutting back might not be as easy as either of you had thought. Firing your live-in handyman could cause an unanticipated eviction for nonpayment of rent.

Here is where a lease is mandatory. You have created two relationships, tenant and handyman. When you terminate one relationship, it will have an impact on the other relationship. Outlining the relationship in writing before you hire him will help. Still, you will have to defend both relationships in housing court if the tenant cannot or refuses to pay the full rent.

You might also have your other tenants taking sides. If they liked him as the handyman, they will resent his firing, unless it was for something that had an impact on them. If they did not like the handyman, well, he knows their secrets. Either way, he might decide he has a chance at fighting the eviction.

Before you begin any action, go over your duties as a landlord and employer of the former handyman. Review any potential problem that might come up in court. Do "the courtroom test," discussed in the box in Chapter 4. If you paid money or forgave all or a portion of the rent, did you declare the rent he did not have to pay as his income to the IRS with a 1099 form for each year of service? If you are hesitant about anything, contact an attorney or accountant before going to court.

DOMESTIC VIOLENCE

A rental homeowner should get involved with a tenant experiencing domestic violence when the problem spills out into the public area with fights, furniture crashing, and repeated damage to the property. Evicting the tenant used to be the resolution until 2005, when it was determined by the federal government that women disproportionately suffer domestic violence more often than men.

H.R. 3402, the "Violence Against Women and Department of Justice Reauthorization Act of 2005, (VAWA)" is a federal law that has important new protections for victims of domestic violence, dating violence, or stalking. This law protects victims living in public housing or using federal housing vouchers anywhere in the country. Many states also have laws that give housing rights to victims of domestic violence, dating violence, sexual assault, or stalking.[11]

The primary reason for this law is to protect the tenant, usually a woman, from being evicted because of an unwanted guest or visitor to the property. The tenant becomes the victim when a boyfriend or spouse, whether an "ex" or not, attacks the tenant in her own home, creating a violation of the quiet enjoyment lease provision. To the degree that this type of violence is more often directed against women, it presents a form of sexual discrimination to evict, covered under the Title VIII Federal Fair Housing Act of 1968.[12]

If you are dealing with a Section 8 tenant, this law will affect your eviction. Do your research before sending a notice to quit to your Section 8 tenant you want to evict because of domestic violence and stalking issues. For a summary of the Violence Against Women Act, go to the National Network to End Domestic Violence Web site at **www.nnedv.org/policy/issues/ vawa.html.**

ELDERLY, HANDICAPPED, AND/OR INFIRM

Some homeowners will balk at evicting the elderly, disabled, or handicapped. Unfortunately, the time might arrive when you have to decide that eviction is the only answer for that tenant. Running a business can sometimes be unpleasant, and evicting an elderly or disabled person is nasty business. Still, the same question remains: how bad does your situation have to get before you decide that it is time for your rent-delinquent tenant to leave? How bad does the damage done to your apartment have to get before you decide to take legal action?

Anyone would be upset if a landlord tried to evict his or her mother or father from an apartment. The reason would not matter. It would be infuriating that a landlord would try to evict an elderly woman from a home she has known for more than, let us say, ten to 20 years. Expect the tenant's family to be angry.

Why evict an elderly person if the rent is paid on time every month? Perhaps an elderly tenant can no longer care for him or herself in the apartment without extra help. Perhaps small fires have been set when the tenant forgot a pan was on the stove. The tenant might even call and ask you to do things that a personal care attendant should do. The family members might not be able or willing to accept this information. They might not be in a position to help the tenant every day.

The reasons will vary — alcoholism, fire damage, dementia, incontinence, and hoarding are examples. All due to chronic, offensive circumstances that create an environment so intolerable to either the property or the other tenants that legal action is the only course to pursue. No matter how fond you are of the tenant, one day, it might be his or her time to leave the property.

When you know that eviction of an elderly tenant is inevitable, you should use extra care to either try to resolve the problem or find a mutually acceptable arrangement for the tenant to move out. Consideration should be made for the age of the tenant, how long he or she has lived in the property, the extent of the problem, and whether the tenant has outside resources to assist in resolving the situation.

It is always comforting if you know you did everything possible to prevent the move-out. Consider these issues if nonpayment of rent is not a concern:

- Is the tenant a danger to herself, the building, or both?

- Is the tenant coherent enough to discuss the problem(s) with you?

- Are the tenant's children or friends currently involved with the tenant?

- Is the tenant's family disinterested about the problem?

- Does the tenant have a healthcare provider?

- Have you notified the emergency contact person on your resident emergency contact information form?

Evicting an elderly or infirm tenant will require tight, detailed documentation. Your case must demonstrate that you did whatever you could to prevent legal action. You must convince the judge that repossession of the apartment is essential for the good of the property.

TENANT IN THE MILITARY

Before you begin eviction procedures against your tenant, you need to make sure that no member of the family is on active duty in the military. It could influence your ability to evict. It will influence how your eviction will be processed.

When the Iraq War sent thousands of Army Reservists and National Guard servicemen and women overseas, it also left a financial gap for those left at home. Extended service duty further affected the military person's private life, particularly in those instances where the primary breadwinner was no longer at home. The family members remaining at home could be in the position of living from military pay as their sole income. The federal government realized that it needed to protect those military personnel who had to drop their private civilian lives and income at a moment's notice to serve their country.

The Servicemembers Civil Relief Act of 2003 (SCRA), amended in 2004, was enacted to protect active-duty military personnel, their spouses, and dependents from foreclosure, evictions, and other financial consequences of serving in the military.[13]

This Act specifically protects a member in the military who is ordered to leave a station or to deploy for 90 days or more. Verification of such is available from the commanding officer, with respect to the member's current or future military duty status.

The SCRA allows military members to terminate their leases upon entry into military service or a change of permanent station. This protection extends to joint leases. The eviction court must find the service member's failure to pay rent is not materially affected by his or her military service.

Material effect is present when the service member does not earn sufficient income to pay the rent. When the member is materially affected by military service, the court may stay the eviction (three months unless the court decides on a shorter or longer period in the interest of justice) when the military member or dependents request it.

There is no requirement that the lease be entered into before entry on active duty, and the court could make any other just order. The requirements of this section are: (1) The landlord is attempting eviction during a period in which the service member is in military service or after receipt of orders to report to duty; (2) the rented premises are used for housing by the spouse, children, or other dependents of the service member; and (3) the agreed rent does not exceed $2,465 per month (in 2004. This amount increases each year with inflation). Source: the Department of the Army.

If a default judgment is entered against a service member during his or her active duty service or within 60 days thereafter, the SCRA allows the military member to reopen that default judgment and set it aside. In order to set aside a default judgment, the service member must show that he or she was prejudiced by not being able to appear in person and that he or she has good and legal defenses to the claims against him or her. The military member must apply to the court for relief in 90 days of the termination or release from military service.

If you have discovered that your tenant is in the military, it might be prudent to get counsel from a housing attorney. A good attorney familiar with The Servicemembers Civil Relief Act of 2003 (SCRA) will ensure that you and the tenant are protected as you process your case in accordance with federal guidelines.

11

DO YOU HAVE A "LEGAL" APARTMENT?

The circular argument heard in court when rent is withheld for lack of repairs is the same. Both parties are holding out for the other to do something before he or she will act on what the other person wants. The tenant says, "I'm not paying my rent because I need repairs completed." The landlord says, "I'm not completing repairs until I get the rent."

The other, more prevalent argument will be the tenant stating that his or her apartment is not "legal." This arises when a homeowner builds a basement apartment without the benefit of obtaining a building permit from the city. If this is true, you had better take care of that problem before you start any eviction proceedings. If a tenant ever calls the city housing inspection department or building department to see whether the apartment is legal, that inspector will call a halt to this tenancy.

REVIEW YOUR LEASE

Your lease could be legally outdated, due to state revisions or updates in law. You should also verify that your addenda are legal.

A lease outlines what a tenant can and cannot do in the apartment, when, and how. This is one of the first pieces of documentation to review before you start any legal action. If your lease does not cover a violation for which you want to evict, this could pose a problem.

The best time to review your lease is before the tenant signs it. To prevent any misunderstanding about what you want the tenant to do or not do in your apartment, include or add those clauses to the lease.

If more than one person signed your lease, you must send the legal eviction notice to each person who signed. This includes a copy to the co-signer and the local housing authority, if you have a Section 8 tenant.

If you do not have a lease with the tenant, you need to check with your state statutes for the time periods, wording, and type of notice required to terminate the tenancy. Your lease should give the amount of notice required to terminate the tenancy. The time depends on the nature of the violation. Check the laws in your state.

Find out whether you have an "unenforceable" lease. This is a lease that is so out of date that the laws have changed significantly since you and your tenant signed it. If you have clauses or additions that are illegal or cannot be pursued in a court of law, you need to know before you go to court. A real estate attorney can advise you whether you have a legally enforceable lease.

Suppose you begin your eviction action, only to find out that you cannot pursue it because your basement apartment is not zoned for occupancy. The judge will not evict a tenant from an illegal apartment. You have to stop the eviction process until your paperwork and your illegal apartment are in order. Worse, the tenant could stop paying the rent, stating it is not a "legal apartment."

You are responsible as the owner or manager for ensuring that all your apartments are in compliance with the laws and ordinances of the state. You can prevent many complaints and potential eviction fights by keeping your apartment and building in good working order.

One way to make sure your building is in good condition is to conduct a monthly building inspection and an apartment inspection every six months. It is always prudent to get the tenant to sign any apartment inspection you conduct in the unit. Sample forms are in the Appendix. Inspections should always be committed to writing. A work order for each needed repair should be written up for your handyman or contractor to complete.

RENT-CONTROLLED APARTMENT

Rent control is a mandatory rental program run by local or state governments that regulates the amount of rent a landlord can charge.

If your property is located in a city with rent-control laws, you will have several extra steps to your eviction case before you can go to court. You need to get the rent-control laws and ordinances and research your obligations as a building owner, because you need permission in housing court from the city rent-control board to evict your tenant.

Rent-controlled apartments must be registered with the city in which the property is located. Failure to register each apartment in the building will seriously delay your eviction case by months. If you failed to register your apartments with rent control and increased rents during the time you were not registered, rent control may force you to roll back all unauthorized rent increases before it will hear your case. This is why you need to keep abreast of the renting laws in your city and state.

CERTIFICATE OF OCCUPANCY

A certificate of occupancy is a document that says your apartment has been renovated, repaired, or fixed up in accordance with the state building code. This document is often mandatory for a new or renovated building issued by, and in accordance with, the state building department. You can go to your state building department to get evidence that your property was issued a certificate of occupancy. Have a copy for your permanent records.

This is important. If your certificate says your building is composed of two three-bedroom apartments and does not say there is an additional room or apartment in the basement, you have an eviction problem. Once the tenant says he lives in "the basement apartment" and you are asked for your copy of the certificate of occupancy, your eviction is stopped until you get proof.

Some city or state jurisdictions require a city inspector to go through your vacant apartment and certify it as "habitable" before you can rent it out again. A fee must be paid for the service, which provides you with a level of protection that shows that when your tenant moved into your apartment, it was safe for occupancy.

Check your city's housing ordinances at your city hall to see whether your area has such a law before renting out your unit.

LEAD PAINT CERTIFICATE

Has your property been de-leaded, both inside and outside of the entire house or building? If yes, you should have a written lead paint certificate. How long ago was it completed? If you have a lead paint certificate that is several years old, you need to see if it is still current. If you have flaking or chipping paint on the outside of your house, you might have to renew or update your lead paint certificate with the city.

You should inform your tenant(s) that the building is not de-leaded before giving out a lease and keys. This might become an issue, if not the issue, of an eviction. For example, your tenant's three-year-old daughter has tested positive for lead. The tenant has decided not to pay the rent until you have de-leaded the apartment and common areas. If you have proof that you have a current certificate of de-leading, produce it. If you cannot prove that the area occupied by the tenant is de-leaded, you could be asked to have it de-leaded before you can proceed with the eviction, and the tenant might be able to avoid paying the rent until it is de-leaded.

FIRE ESCAPE AND EXTINGUISHER CERTIFICATES

If you have fire extinguishers in the apartments and/or the public hallway, they should be inspected and updated every year. When you do your annual apartment inspection, include a look at the condition of the fire extinguisher, the smoke detectors, and the carbon monoxide detectors. In New Jersey in 2005, a law passed that every apartment in a three-unit or fewer building must have a portable fire extinguisher.[14]

There are states, such as Massachusetts, that require a building owner to maintain a metal or wooden fire escape in mint condition on a regular basis. In the case of a fire escape in Massachusetts, the state requires that the fire department issue a certificate of inspection every five years. Your state building code or fire escape code will provide you with information on the laws of your state.

If you have a wood or metal fire escape at any of your properties and have never had it inspected for compliance or for the integrity of the structure, you can expect to pay heavy fines or have legal action taken against you if your fire escape fails to work or falls down if there is a fire in your building. Also expect your insurance company to fight with you over paying fines; you could find it difficult to defend whatever liabilities are incurred due to your neglect.

The same thing applies to porches. Regardless of whether you must file a certificate of integrity, your tenant could decide not to pay the rent because of your failure to keep your porches in good repair. In the worst-case scenario, a tenant or visitor to the property could have a serious injury, even a wrongful death suit, because of a poorly maintained fire extinguisher, fire escape, smoke detector, or porch.

When you sign a contractor to repair or replace a porch or fire escape, make sure the contractor can pull a building permit. Also, have the vendor give you a copy of the company's certificate of insurance, both liability and workers' compensation. You want to be protected if in the process of repairing or replacing your fire escape, your contractor's insurance is sued if anyone is hurt on your property, including a tenant who might trip and fall over some wood or metal pole.

IS YOUR PROPERTY MAINTAINED?

As a landlord, it is your duty to maintain the property in a manner that will keep your tenants happy. What kind of landlord are you when it comes to making repairs? What are your policies on making building and tenant repairs? Your attitude toward repairs and maintenance of your property might be an issue in your eviction case.

- Did you fix up and paint the apartment before the tenant first moved in?

- Does it take weeks before you get around to fixing something in your tenant's apartment?

- Does your tenant call the housing inspector about needed repairs before calling you? Is the tenant doing it because you have a history of not responding to repair requests?

- Do you have a policy of not making repairs until the item needs to be replaced?

- Do you constantly say you do not have the money to make repairs but come up with it after the housing inspector calls?

- Have you tried to fix housing or building code violations before taking the tenant to court? Did the tenant cooperate by allowing you in the apartment to make the repairs? Can you prove noncompliance by the tenant?

- When was the last time you saw the inside of your tenant's apartment?

Before you start eviction action, know that some of the habits exhibited above could go against you in court. It could show a history of not maintaining the property or keeping it up to the state building or sanitary codes. If you do not have a properly maintained building or apartment, expect the tenant to go to court with pictures of your property as a defense for not paying the rent.

A poorly maintained property or apartment could have a serious impact on your eviction case. Some judges will not continue your case until a city housing inspector surveys the tenant's apartment and the building. Any repair or other issues, such as a need for pest control, will stop your eviction. Until the city and state building code violations are corrected, your eviction case is held for further consideration.

After you make the repairs, you are responsible for calling the housing inspector for another inspection of the property. If all is well, then ask for a new court date.

Review Your Insurance Policy

While you are going over all your legal records, this would be a good time to review your homeowner's insurance policy. It is a large document that most people just file away. Read it one day.

You might be surprised to see what your policy covers and does not cover. Do not wait until you are sued to go through your policy, only to find it does not cover the lawsuit problem.

Property management companies with large real estate portfolios have an insurance person who visits all the properties. The goal is to examine each building for potential insurance liabilities. The property manager is then instructed to cure every violation that would void the insurance policy. The insurance examiner returns to each property and signs off that the work has been completed.

You might think this is not necessary for your two- or three-family home, but it is better to pay for an insurance liability inspection than to defend against a tenant lawsuit asking for thousands of dollars.

12 DOCUMENT THE PROBLEM

All eviction cases are decided based on facts proved by visual, written, or audiotaped evidence. You must prove your claim to your apartment and prove that your tenant broke the lease or behaved in such a way that he or she must vacate. Make sure that the eviction is based on solid legal ground. If you are suing for nonpayment of rent, you will need to produce a record of payments and charges. If you want to reclaim your apartment because of specific negative behavior that is having an impact on your property, you must prove what was done and how it is affecting your unit or the building.

It is difficult in court to explain what happened to cause the eviction. People get emotional, forget details, and/or talk out of turn. A judge likes to see written, verbal, or visual evidence of the problem. You will be expected to give the judge written examples of why you want the tenant evicted. You should have begun to document your case weeks or months before sending the eviction notice. There are times when, if you document the problem and give it to the tenant, it could make the situation real to him or her. You might be able to prevent an eviction just by notifying your tenant there is a problem between you.

The Incident Report

Whenever there are problems with a tenant or between tenants, in the property management profession, we complete what is called an incident or property report. You should also complete an incident report when something out of the ordinary happens at the building. This is a form of documentation that will help you not only with an eviction case, but it could also assist with a property liability case filed against you by a tenant or visitor to the property.

During the passing of time, your tenant might exhibit a host of negative behaviors. Over a six-month time period, when you are finally ready to evict the tenant, how will you remember every atrocity committed? You need a formal method of getting the behavior in writing at the time it happens.

Make sure you put every complaint about the tenant in writing. Keep a copy for your records in the tenant's file folder. Just state the facts. Do not exaggerate. Let the problem speak for itself. Document the following information:

- When — date, day, and time of the incident

- What happened?

- Where did the incident happen? In the apartment? In the hallway? Outside?

- How long did the problem go on?

- Who and how many people were involved?

- Were the police called? Fire department?

- Who reported the information? Did you observe this yourself?

PREVENTIVE ANTICIPATION — INCIDENT REPORTS

While you were in the front of your building in the Northeast, throwing down rock salt on the sidewalk in November, you saw your tenant slip on the ice going to her car. You had already spread rock salt and sand on that area of the sidewalk. Fortunately, she did not fall, and you remember you said, "Watch out," as she slid around before catching herself. When you finished spreading the rock salt and sand, you went inside and typed a note about the incident. You noted the day, time, the date, and jotted down what happened. You put the note in your tenant's file folder in your file cabinet.

In January the next year, you receive a letter from your tenant's attorney. It states that on the day in question, your tenant slipped and fell on the sidewalk. It was covered with ice, and the tenant sprained her ankle and has incurred substantial medical bills and time out from work. The attorney is asking for an undisclosed amount of money for punitive, legal, and medical damages.

You make a copy of the attorney's letter and send it to your insurance company. You also send a copy of the incident report you made on the day in question. It provides valuable information to your insurance company about what happened that day. The case is litigated between the attorneys with little fanfare. Your insurance rate does not go up when you renew your policy.

Letter or E-mail

There are times when you need to send a letter to the tenant. The purpose is to explain a problem that has been brought to your attention and what the tenant needs to do about it. This is your first defense toward documenting, if not preventing, a potential legal problem.

The letter should be brief, factual, to the point, and clear. You do not have to write much. Just state the facts. Quote what part of the lease has been violated and what you want done about the situation. Do not make any promises in writing. You may not be able to do what you said you would do in your e-mail. Keep a copy for your records in the tenant file.

Save e-mails and text messages, both sent and received. Be careful what you write. Your tenant is saving your e-mails and text messages, too. One moment of anger, some curse words, a veiled threat or two, and not only might your case disappear, the tenant could file a counter suit for harassment.

Here is an example of the kind of letter you might send to your tenant:

EXAMPLE LETTER
Dear Mr. Smith:
It has been brought to my attention that on Saturday, August 4, 2004, you had a party in your apartment that lasted until 3 a.m. Your visitors were very loud as they left the building, shouting and arguing in the vestibule and front doorway. This is the second time you have had a party in the past two months that has lasted until the early morning hours and that your visitors were excessively loud while leaving the building. I thought we agreed the last time we spoke that you would cooperate with the other tenants in the building by ending your parties by midnight.

EXAMPLE LETTER

Section 3, Article 2 of your lease states that "excessive noise that disturbs the quiet enjoyment of other tenants is not allowed." Please review your lease and consider your neighbors in the future by asking your visitors to keep their voices low when they leave your apartment and the building. And please respect our agreement to end any party in your apartment by midnight.

I hope that this letter will not be necessary to write again. If you wish to discuss this with me, I can be reached at 617-555-2312.

Sincerely,
Robert Thomas
Landlord

cc: Leased Housing Depart. (If the tenant holds a Section 8 certificate or voucher)

NEIGHBORHOOD WATCH

Find out whether your street is part of a neighborhood watch group. This is a preventive mechanism where homeowners monitor their streets and neighbors for suspicious and/or illegal activities. At neighborhood watch monthly meetings, the residents report who is doing what and later report those happenings to the police. The goal is to keep its neighborhood free from crime, intrusive noise, hangout buildings, and drug dealing. There might be signs on street light poles indicating the street has a community patrol looking out for suspicious or illegal activities.

As a homeowner, you should always be on friendly terms with your neighbors, especially the next-door neighbors on either side of your property. They can tell you what goes on when you are not home.

A formal neighborhood watch group meets with the local police department on a monthly basis. Contact the officer in charge of the monthly community meetings and find out whether there have been reports about activities at your property. If a police report has been filed complaining about actions at your house, get a copy of the report.

Find out whether your local police department has crime prevention meetings around your neighborhood. This is where the police inform residents about problems they have had with drinking, teenagers, and car thefts. They also discuss plans they have to address the problem(s). The police also want to hear about things going on of which they are not aware.

At the crime watch meetings, residents provide information such as license plate numbers, descriptions of "regulars" who hang out on the street but do not live there, and the days and times when suspicious behaviors happen.

You should seriously consider being an active member of your neighborhood watch. There are powerful watches that have been able to move illegal or non-productive activities from their neighborhoods. As a homeowner, you owe it to yourself and your real estate investment to ensure that your street and property do not become a harbor for tenants and/or loiterers conducting illegal behaviors.

Be aware that at these crime watch meetings, you might hear about what is going on at your own house. Homeowners will come to the meetings with specific information that could tremendously help your case, such as dates, times, who did what, and what happened. On the one hand, that is information you will need to begin and continue your eviction case, but on the other, you might be confronted and asked why you have not taken action sooner. You might also be asked to give regular progress records on your eviction action.

ARE YOU ON TOP OF REPAIRS?

Suppose your tenant calls you on a Wednesday, around 11 p.m., and says her bathroom faucet is leaking. What do you do? Is it dripping or running? Can it wait until the morning? If you have to go to work the next day, how will you get the leak fixed? What if the tenant will not be home? It does not matter.

You own the property; you have to make the repair in a timely manner. The hook becomes what is considered timely for you, and what is considered timely for the tenant. This could be an issue in court.

Lack of timely responses to maintenance requests is often a counterclaim of a tenant under eviction. The tenant needs to be assured that you will take service requests seriously and will take care of them in the next few days. Emergencies should be completed the same day. If a tenant says she has not paid the rent because of outstanding repairs she requested, that could extend your eviction case.

Track when requests come in, when the work has been scheduled, and when it is completed. Use the work order request form in the Appendix to document requests for repairs from your tenants. Have the tenant sign the request as proof of satisfaction with the repair(s).

SMALL-CLAIMS COURT

Some issues can be solved without going to eviction court.

There are some states that will not allow a homeowner to take a tenant to small-claims court before the tenant moves out. If you believe that there are damages that will exceed the amount of the security deposit in the bank, inform the court clerk to see if you can still file. If your tenant vandalized the refrigerator you provided, to the point where you have to have it replaced, the tenant must pay for it.

Suppose your tenant allowed her 4-year-old son to drop his GI Joe down the toilet. You had to have a plumber remove the toilet, get out the toy, replace the wax seal, and put the toilet back. You were charged $75 for the service. This fee should be billed to the tenant. Give him or her 30 days to pay the bill. After that time has passed, take the tenant to small-claims court.

The Appendix has an example of a form you can copy and then send to any tenant who has damaged the apartment or equipment. I call it the resident damage letter, because it documents what was done to the apartment, how much it cost to have it fixed, and when you want to be paid. It also tells the tenant what will happen if the damages are not paid by the date.

KEEP SECTION 8 INFORMED

Your Section 8 lease is not only with the tenant, but the federal government, too. Section 8 is also your tenant. This means that whatever you do to evict your Section 8 tenant, you need to inform the Section 8 administrator at the same time. This includes letters, eviction notices, and when you reserve any of your legal rights during the eviction process. A copy of any and all letters and legal correspondence should always go to the Section 8 Leasing Officer for the tenant.

Failure to notify the Section 8 people during the legal process could cost you your ability to evict the tenant. Read the Section 8 lease before you start an eviction to make sure you comply with its regulations. If you do not, you might be forced to start all over again.

The Section 8 Leasing Officer may contact you regarding the eviction on behalf of its tenant. If the issue is rent arrears, the leasing officer may offer a partial rent payment in lieu of eviction action. Be careful that you do not give up your right to continue the eviction until all of your rent is paid in full.

13 MAKE YOUR DECISION, THEN STICK TO IT

You might be wondering whether you should take the family's situation into consideration. Perhaps the mother is pregnant. Maybe the father lost his job and has not been able to get another one that pays enough to cover rent as well as his other obligations. You might feel sorry for the tenant and not take legal action for a month or two.

Taking care of the income and expenses of a rental income property is business. Paying the mortgage on time every month to avoid foreclosure is your responsibility. When rent is unpaid, it might never be recovered. Or, you could recover only a partial amount of what the tenant owed you by the end of the eviction process.

You cannot be afraid to put someone out of your house or building. You must do what must be done for the good of the property, even if the tenant is a close friend or relative. Do not listen to your tenant's sob stories. If you listen to your tenant's story, remain openly firm about continuing the eviction. Once you decide to begin legal action, follow through to the end. If you stop, you might have to start all over again. If you keep changing your mind about whether you will evict the tenant, you send the tenant the message that you can be manipulated.

Let me explain why it is necessary to steel yourself when you decide to put the tenant out of your apartment. Homelessness is a problem in the United States. Even if your tenant has a job, he or she could have a problem finding another apartment within the time of your eviction process.

A city with a housing shortage will affect your ability to get a court judgment without plenty of good evidence and facts to support your case. The judge will know that once he or she grants an eviction, the tenant will have a hard time finding somewhere else to live. The chance that your tenant with a family of three or more children will be homeless is great, if you live in a city with a low vacancy rate.

Rents in a city with a housing shortage tend to be higher than average for a vacant apartment. This is because the supply is low, and the demand for units is great. If your tenant has to move into another apartment, he or she will have to come up with the first month's rent, sometimes the last month's rent, and a security deposit. If the rent for a new apartment costs $800, that is $2,400 the tenant needs to move, plus the cost of a moving truck. If the tenant had that kind of money, you would not have to evict for nonpayment of rent.

How Bad is the Problem?

You have given your tenant what you believe is every opportunity to either get the rent current or stop the behavior that is affecting the quiet enjoyment of the property by other tenants. The tenant has broken every rent payment agreement he or she has made with you, or the excessive foot traffic continues nonstop and your other tenants are threatening to move out when their lease expires.

Let us say you are a timid or new homeowner. You have the mortgage to pay, and you cannot afford a long, drawn-out eviction case. The tenant is making life miserable for you and the other tenants. Still, you are reluctant to sue the tenant because you are afraid that if you do, he or she could stop paying the rent. You cannot afford not to have the rent every month. You need to ask yourself these questions:

- Has the tenant problem changed your quality of life or that of your other tenants?

- Can you live with the situation for another month, in hope that the tenant will change? Do you think the tenant will change his or her behavior if you talk to him or her one more time?

- How bad does it have to get before you will take action?

- Why do you keep changing your mind about putting out the tenant?

- Is the tenant a friend or relative, and are you afraid of losing the relationship if you evict?

- What would have to happen before you would take legal action to get control of your apartment again?

- If you had enough money saved up to be able to keep paying the mortgage and evict the tenant, would you?

- What is the worst thing that could happen if you evicted this tenant?

- What is the best thing that could happen if you evicted this tenant?

Use this list as your measurement of how serious you are about the eviction. Go through this list and be honest with your answers. At some point, you will be forced to put your money where your mind and situation is, and you need to be clear about what you want.

A scenario: the tenant has a new baby that does not sleep; therefore, she cries at all hours of the day and night. The tenant who lives below is complaining that he works nights, and the baby's crying is keeping him awake during the day. What will you do?

Here is a different scenario. The tenant upstairs has started to take in children to baby-sit. One is a baby that is about two months old and cries whenever it wants. The tenant below complains that not only does the baby keep him up, but the other children playing and wrestling around during the day is keeping him awake as well.

The first situation with the crying baby is temporary and a part of living in a family building. The baby will cry less as he or she grows older. The second scenario is an illegal day care set up without your written approval. Here you have legal and insurance issues to consider. The danger of allowing the situation to continue is more serious.

Do not be intimidated by your tenant. Do not allow your tenant to bully you into being too afraid to evict. This is your house, your real estate investment. If you have a tenant who is jeopardizing your home and financial investment, ask the tenant to leave. If he or she refuses to leave, use the court system to handle the matter.

IS IT THE MONEY, THE PRINCIPLE, OR THE TENANT?

Expect the rent to stop once you start your eviction. If evicting for nonpayment of rent, this will be no surprise. If you are evicting for bad behavior or lease violations, the tenant may stop paying the rent to save up for his or her next apartment.

Regardless of the reason, the tenant is not paying the rent, and you want it paid. In one situation, you have a Section 8 tenant, and you are getting $1,200 per month for rent. Of that amount, the tenant is paying 30 percent of her income, or $75 a month. That means that the government is paying you $1,125 per month for your apartment.

If the tenant is not paying his or her share of the Section 8 rent, and the subsidy is paying most of the rent, you should still care whether the tenant is paying the tenant share of the rent.

Either you are in business or running a charity operation. You asked for $1,200 a month, and now you are settling for less. Consequently, that is what you will always get — less than what you want or need.

If Section 8 finds out that you are not collecting the full rent from the tenant, it can reduce your total rent by that much. This is because the federal government is a business, too. It does not want to pay more for rent than anyone else, either. When you have to renew your Rental Assistance Contract, it will reduce your total rent by $75. Then, you will receive only $1,125 per month total.

If this tenant stops paying the rent, she will brag about it to the other tenants in the building. They will not appreciate your allowing one tenant not to pay the rent, while you collect the full rent from the rest of the tenants. Next, you will have two tenants not paying the rent and a third one paying late each month.

A tenant who stops paying the rent often has other problems. If she cannot pay $75 a month, she might be spending her income on luxuries or nonessentials. If you make her pay the rent after a few months of nonpayment, her new spending habits will conflict with your new rent policy, and she may think she can get away with other things, too.

If you recognize that the next place your tenant is going may be a shelter, does that change your mind about pursuing legal action? Even if the tenant is your niece, with your 2-year-old great-niece, and the rent has not been paid for two months, that should not change your mind.

You are not evicting the tenant; the tenant's behavior is evicting him or her. Regardless of the circumstances or the person, your lease has been broken. You either have rules, or you do not. I have had to evict tenants and families that I liked. When I was an employee, I had to evict relatives of my supervisors or boss. I could not and did not play favorites. That would have been to the detriment of the other tenants and the building and my reputation as a fair and impartial manager.

Rent pays the bills. Tenants pay rent. Anything that jeopardizes those two elements must be dealt with to keep your property on a paying basis. Once you decide to file for an eviction, keep going to its conclusion. If it is for rent, you want the money. If it is for a nuisance problem, you want the apartment back.

EXPECT THE TENANT TO BE ANGRY AND UPSET

No one wants to be evicted or have his or her belongings thrown or placed in boxes, taken away to a storage warehouse, or put out on the street. If the tenant is related to you or has been your friend, he or she should not have put you in this position. If the tenant has been recently divorced or lost a job, that is a situation that will not be soon rectified or have a quick recovery. Still, without the rent, you will soon be in a difficult situation also.

Even if your mortgage has been paid in full, you need the rent for expenses, real estate taxes, the water bill, maintenance, and other expenses. You live off the income of the property, and you might need the income from that property for your retirement income. By not paying the rent, your tenant is trying to live off your property, too. Do not let that person or family do that to you.

Expect the tenant to be angry or upset with you for taking eviction action. You can explain that it is nothing personal, just business, but expect resentment. You will have an especially difficult eviction if the tenant is a friend or relative.

DO NOT TRADE WORK FOR RENT

The tenant may suggest that he do some work on the property

159

in lieu of paying the rent arrears. This is a bad suggestion, and I would not advise you allow it. This creates another relationship. If it does not work out, it will be a difficult eviction. Each of you will feel betrayed by the other.

14 THINGS YOU CANNOT DO TO YOUR TENANT

Before you decide to take legal action — and sometimes during the eviction process, you might be tempted to do things to the tenant to force him or her to comply with your rules, to pay the rent, or to move out — but you cannot attempt to rush the eviction process by taking matters into your own hands and helping yourself out of your problems with your tenant(s).

Frustration, anger, desperation, and lack of finances are some situations that could drive you to behave badly. If you try to go head-to-head with a tenant, you could come out the loser. Below are some actions or behaviors that I have encountered from landlords driven to the brink of madness and unaware that they were in violation of the law.

DO NOT PLAY GAMES

Eviction is serious business. It is a power struggle, with a winner and a loser. The loser could have small children and become homeless. Do not make a game out of constantly threatening the tenant when you do not intend to evict the person. If you want the apartment in order to move in your sister, say it and do it.

Do not use a flimsy excuse to get a tenant to move out. It could come back against you.

If you constantly make threats but never follow up, the tenant could start to believe you are merely trying to harass him or her out of the apartment, instead of using the legal system. There are too many legal ways to move out a tenant. Say what you mean, and mean what you say, or be quiet and leave the tenant alone.

DO NOT CHANGE THE LOCKS

Your tenant owes you at least two month's rent. This is making you angry, especially when you see that the tenant has just installed a washing machine in her apartment. You feel that if she can afford that, she should be able to pay the rent. You decide to take action and send a message to your tenant by changing the locks to her apartment.

Changing the locks to your tenant's apartment without advance notice or good cause is considered a "constructive" eviction, or an illegal lockout. This means that you caused the tenant to have to move elsewhere, even if for a few hours, because you prevented him or her from being able to enter the apartment. It is an illegal act, and harsh punishments are given to the housing owner for this type of self-help.

An illegal eviction could cost you three times the cost of damages you incur by tossing out your tenant without a court order. The only lock-out you are legally able to perform is one where a judge has provided you with an eviction document and you had a constable or sheriff move the tenant out in accordance with the laws of your state. Check your state laws regarding penalties on homeowners for inappropriate behavior toward a tenant.

Do not change any lock to your tenant's apartment. If the tenant has two locks, and you change one of them just to aggravate the tenant, this is considered an illegal activity. If you change the front entry door lock and fail to give your tenant under eviction a key, this is also constructive eviction and illegal. These two examples could also be considered harassment. Take the tenant to court instead.

Do not change any apartment lock until the tenant has either obviously abandoned the apartment or has been legally evicted by the sheriff or constable.

DO NOT ENTER THE APARTMENT WITHOUT ADVANCE NOTICE

There is a distinct line between checking on the property and being a nosy or intrusive landlord. Once you have rented out your apartment, that space belongs to the tenant. You cannot go in and out of the unit without good cause. Your tenants have rights, such as being able to use the apartment in peace without you going in and out of it at will.

Do not violate your tenants' rights and/or their rights to privacy. Your lease should cover the fact that unless it is an emergency, you will not go into the tenant's apartment without giving advance notice.

Do not go into your tenant's apartment before or after sending the eviction notice to "collect evidence" or to "see if they are still there." It is against the law to enter your tenant's apartment without their consent or if there is not an emergency. This is considered trespassing or breaking and entering.

The eviction notice is just the start of the eviction process. You should have documented your case well before you decided to evict. Whatever you did not do or have beforehand will have to stay undone. Do not try to "create" an emergency situation so that you can gain entry. Stay out of the tenant's apartment during the eviction process. It is not yours yet.

Stay Away From the Tenant

A tenant with a fatal attraction to his 65-year-old female landlord tries to kill her when he receives his eviction notice. A landlord and tenant get into a fistfight after the landlord approaches his tenant to ask for the rent. An 80-year-old landlord is hit in the head with a frying pan when his tenant, under eviction, breaks into his home.

These are true examples of what can happen when an eviction goes wrong. An eviction is just as infuriating for the tenant as it is for you. You never know how a tenant will react to an eviction notice. Some will not go quietly. It is best not to add fuel to the fire by engaging the tenant in conversation until you get to court.

Never use harassment as a means of collecting rent. Use the court system. Once you have filed your eviction action, there should not be much to say to the tenant. There is no reason to continue to engage in conversation about a situation that could not be resolved before you spent your money filing for eviction. Calling the tenant every other day asking when the rent will be paid is asking for trouble.

Your tenant is already in a tough spot. You have served the tenant with potential homelessness. Do not add to the problem by continuing to make life miserable for him or her. Do not behave like a juvenile, no matter how angry you are with the tenant. Sending a dozen pizzas to the apartment every Saturday night will only get you in trouble.

Do not Google the tenant to get his or her e-mail address and then send threatening e-mails. Do not send an e-mail a day asking for the rent. File your eviction case, and let the justice system work. Any e-mail you send will be used against you by the tenant in court. Do not give your tenant the written ammunition to dilute your case. You should keep all e-mails sent to you by the tenant. Do not decide which ones will benefit your case and throw away the others; bring all of them to court.

Also, do not threaten the tenant, either openly or by subtle messages. It is not funny to say to a tenant, "I hope your cat Fluffy does not get lost while he's in the hallway." This is a veiled threat to imply that you will let Fluffy out the door the next time you find it in the public hallway. If anything were to happen to the cat after that statement, your tenant could sue you for the loss or claim retaliatory action against you during the eviction case.

Let the legal system work for you, let your attorney do your talking, and let the judge decide the case. Nothing different is going to happen by continuing to talk to your tenant about the situation. The best thing to do until you get to court is to stay away from each other.

SEXUAL HARASSMENT

This is different from "regular" harassment. In this situation, the owner or landlord offers to deduct or forget the rent in exchange for sexual favors. This is a stupid thing to do. When you conduct yourself in this manner, you are offering to perform an illegal act. It is undignified to both you and the tenant. It demonstrates you are not looking at your home as a valid real estate investment. You are also trying to run a business using your personal home or investment property as a brothel.

Leave the tenant alone. You want the rent money, the apartment, or both. Even if you make an obscene offer in a brief moment of lust and then try to forget it happened, the tenant will never forget. The sexual offer will be repeated in court. You will be publicly embarrassed, and you could lose your eviction case because of it.

Sexual entanglement is a different situation. In this case, you and the tenant, who lived in one of your apartments, had a real, mutually agreed romantic relationship that went belly-up. Now you, as the landlord, want her out of your apartment building. What did she do so wrong that she must be evicted? You better have some good reasons, with the proper documentation behind it, or this could turn into a case of retaliation.

Do you want every bit of personal information about you discussed in open court? The tenant will use whatever she has to in order to stay in the apartment until she is ready to go. Every promise, every time you let her slide on the rent for the month, all special work you did in the apartment will all be told. It is an embarrassing thing to see and hear in court.

Your credibility will be torn to shreds, and you will be laughed at, all because you could not leave your tenant alone. Keep business and pleasure separate.

Do Not Call Your Tenant at Work

If you want to antagonize your tenant and make him or her crazy, call at work and ask for the rent. Calling a tenant at work does not accomplish anything, except to make you feel better and aggravate the tenant. Depending on how often you call over the course of days, or even weeks, it could be considered harassment. There are some employers who will terminate an employee for getting excessive personal telephone calls. You do not want to be sued by your tenant because you kept calling at work. If you want your unpaid rent, send the notice to quit and wait the required number of days to send the court hearing notice.

Maintain Your Tenant's Right to Privacy

Do not broadcast to everyone who will listen that you are evicting your tenant. You could be sued for slander, especially if you lose the case. The tenant will be angry that you talked publicly about his or her personal business without the benefit of first taking the matter to court. You cannot win an eviction case by public opinion. Besides, by talking about the case, you could encourage or force people, including the other tenants in the building, to take sides. This might not go in your favor.

When talking to your other tenants, if asked about whether you are evicting one of their neighbors, it is best to be coy about the subject. Tell them that you "cannot confirm or deny" this because of privacy issues. You want your other tenants to feel that you would not violate their privacy and would keep their personal business to yourself.

Even if you win the case, to be on the safe side, keep your victory dance to yourself until the move-out has occurred. An eviction, once completed, becomes a matter of public record. Restrain your urge to flaunt your achievement until the paperwork is finished.

DO NOT TURN OFF THE UTILITIES

Shutting off utilities is considered an act of retaliation. Depending upon the utility you cut off, what you do could also be considered constructive eviction. Either way, the intent is to "encourage" the tenant to move out of your apartment because the basic utility necessities have been removed. This action in some states could cause you to pay triple damages to the tenant.

Judges frown on utility turnoffs. It will not go in your favor if the tenant informs the judge of this situation. If you violate the tenant's right to have utilities, especially heat in the winter, it could have an impact on your eviction case. The judge could dismiss your case as an act of retaliation, and the tenant could still live there and not pay the rent until the utilities are turned back on. The judge could also penalize you with a fine for every day the utilities were not on.

Not having the funds to fix a major utility problem is no excuse not to make the repair, either. As a business owner, it is your responsibility to ensure that everything works in the apartment. If the heating system fails, you are expected to have it immediately replaced. Providing the tenant with a small heater should only be done as a temporary solution for a day or two while the installation is taking place. You cannot use the excuse that you do not have the funds to replace the heating system because the tenant has not paid the rent.

Do not let this happen to you. In fact, you need to take extra care that the telephone wires, cable television, sewer, toilet, smoke detectors, drains, and all other utilities are in working order while your case is pending. The tenant has the right to file a countersuit, showing that you behaved in a manner to cause harm, harassment, inconvenience, or unlawful dispossession before and/or during the eviction process. Do not allow even the appearance that you attempted to harass the tenant to move out before going to court.

DO NOT DISCRIMINATE

You can be sued if you treat one race of tenant or ethnicity differently with your rent policies and court action. Treat everyone the same. If you are strict on one tenant, be strict with all of them. Do not have a policy for some of your tenants and another policy for friends or relatives who live in your building. Make everyone pay the rent on time, and make everyone follow the lease.

If you play favorites with tenants, it will come back to haunt you. Tenants talk to each other. They might even compare notes. A friend or relative to whom you rented an apartment could turn on you during an eviction action. You will go into court, and your "friend" will tell the judge about all the times you played favorites or discriminated against him or her or someone else in the building. The judge will see that you are open to discriminatory behavior, and his or her perception of you will change for the worse.

Playing favorites is not just unfair; it is against federal and state law. The federal Fair Housing Act and Equal Opportunity Act is a law that prosecutes against those who discriminate against any tenant on the basis of Title VIII of the Civil Rights Act of 1968 (Fair Housing Act), as amended, and prohibits discrimination in the sale, rental, and financing of dwellings and in other housing-related transactions, based on race, color, national origin, religion, sex, familial status (including children under the age of 18 living with parents or legal custodians, pregnant women, and people securing custody of children under the age of 18), and handicap (disability).

Title VI of the Civil Rights Act of 1964 prohibits discrimination on the basis of race, color, or national origin in programs and activities receiving federal financial assistance.[15] Some states have added to these acts to include sexual orientation and source of income. The amended state laws have as much authority as the federal laws.

Do Not Help Yourself to Tenant Belongings

Just because you own the building does not give you the right to use your tenant apartment key to conduct some self-help activity. You cannot go into the tenant's apartment and take something of equal value to what you think the tenant owes you. This is called breaking and entering into the apartment, a violation of the law.

I know a homeowner who removed a tenant's computer and held it for ransom, presumably until the rent was paid. Her daughter wisely advised her mother to call me so that I could tell her why that was a wrong thing to do. After we discussed the matter and her options, the mother decided she would quickly return the computer to the tenant's room before she got in from work.

DO NOT USE EVICTION TO RETALIATE

The eviction process is taking too long for you. You are owed two month's rent, you have been trying to carry the mortgage without your tenant's share, and the strain is getting to be too much. You feel betrayed that your best friend's daughter is using you and the relationship between you and her mother to get away with this. You want to do something to let her know who is in charge.

This kind of behavior or action is called "retaliation." Retaliation is another way to "get even" with a tenant. Retaliation is different from the other forms of "self-help" as listed above. What you are doing is "paying back" the tenant for a real or perceived act of vengeance, betrayal, or even for making a legitimate complaint against you.

A retaliation eviction is the most damaging act a homeowner can do to a tenant. It is an act of mean-spiritedness and ill will. It is bad mainly because what a landlord does to get even is often ill conceived. Retaliation could cost you money, more legal action, and maybe a countersuit by the tenant against you. It is the cost of losing your temper and letting your emotions get the best of you over what is a business transaction that did not go your way.

The cost of losing a retaliation case could include paying three times the rent, losing credibility before the judge, possibly losing a friend, and losing the goodwill of a tenant. Let a cool head prevail.

Do Not Refuse to Make Repairs

The eviction process can infuriate a landlord. Let us suppose you rented a nice apartment to someone you thought would be a good tenant for several years. Now, several years later, the tenant is refusing to pay the rent, saying the apartment is a disaster. You decide you will not put any more good money into the apartment until the tenant gets caught up.

Constructive eviction is illegal in just about every state. You cannot refuse to complete needed repairs in the tenant's apartment because he or she owes rent. If you do so, then you are being a negligent homeowner, and you are violating your own lease. When you get to court, the judge will have to decide whether, by failing to maintain the apartment, you were trying to evict the tenant by causing the apartment to fall into disrepair.

This situation consistently grates on the nerve of every client and homeowner. It may be the most common reason why a landlord and tenant are at odds. The owner says, "How can I make repairs without the rent?" The tenant says, "Why should I pay the rent without a repaired apartment?" Regardless of the homeowner's financial situation, failure to provide service to a tenant is not a legal option. This is why a timely eviction suit is the best course of action.

Preventive methods that should be developed before starting an eviction are:

- Decide that you will be a good landlord who maintains a preventive approach to the property instead of a "milk it until it dries up" approach.

- Make repairs before renting the unit; inspect your entire property at least once a year, to see if your apartments are being maintained or vandalized.

- Have the tenant sign off on all completed work, either on a work order, the apartment inspection form, or the vendor's invoice.

- Instead of steaming over a damaged apartment, charge or evict the tenant for excessive damage.

- Raise the rent to keep up with the cost-of-living expenses.

- Make the repairs. If you go to court to evict, the judge is going to make you do the repairs anyway before he gives you the writ of possession.

DO NOT YELL AND SCREAM

There will be times when your tenant will get under your skin during the eviction period. Screaming, yelling, or cursing at the tenant whenever you need to converse with him or her will not help your case. It will not cause the tenant to leave your apartment any faster. It could, however, get you a restraining order from the tenant against you for verbal abuse.

Belittling the tenant, swearing, being sarcastic, calling her names, or talking in a negative way about her children and/or their behavior could also get you in trouble. You are running a real estate business, even if the property is also your home. A professional attitude and a civil tongue will go a long way with the tenant and the court judge.

In addition, your other tenants, seeing that you are a professional person with some class, will deal with you the way they see you deal with a tenant you are evicting. Tenants talk to each other, as well as their friends and neighbors. As your clients, they will either advertise that you are a good landlord under stress or a horrible one who verbally abuses people who cross you. A perceived "bad landlord" will have trouble attracting tenants for vacant apartments.

Finally, everything you say and do to the tenant will be used against you in court. You do not want to be characterized as a raving, screaming lunatic in open court in front of the judge and spectators.

THE RESULT OF VIOLATING THE TENANT'S RIGHTS

There are ramifications to landlords who fail to make repairs, harass tenants and who use retaliatory methods to prompt the tenant to move out. Here are some penalties you might encounter if you decide to fight the system:

- You could be fined and penalized for every day you do not make repairs.

- You will lose Section 8 money as long as the unit fails inspections.

- You can be charged punitive damages of three times the rent.

- The tenant could file a civil lawsuit, stating that you used discriminatory tactics.

- You could lose your original suit because of retaliation and have to start the process over again.

- All of the above could happen to you.

It is easier to just do the repairs, get a tenant signature on every invoice of completed work, and take before-and-after pictures to eviction court.

15 LEGAL TECHNICALITIES

Eviction is a series of legal actions, in chronological order, made promptly and based on written or other evidence that is presented to a court judge. Miss one part of the process, and you can be sent back to start the process over again.

Once you decide to take legal action against your tenant, it does not matter whether you or your lawyer does it; it is going to cost you time, money, and aggravation. You might have to present various parts of your case to more than one city authority figure. Be prepared to spend money to file and pursue your lawsuit. How you choose to file your lawsuit along the eviction process and the extent of your evidence, not hearsay or what you think is going on, will decide how long your eviction will take to complete. Expect the tenant to fight you to the end.

TERMINATION OF TENANCY NOTICE

You must notify your tenant of what you want. You must send a written termination of tenancy, an official notice to quit, to your tenant. This is the first step in the eviction process.

Be careful about paying attention to details of the entire legal process from beginning to end by following the letter of the law in your state. In every case and state, a written notice of termination stating exactly how much rent is due and for which periods of time or the reason(s) that you are filing an eviction must be delivered to the tenant. If it is for a lease violation, you must state which sections or articles of the lease have been broken.

Make sure the notice has correctly spelled the name of each party to the lease. A misspelled name could force you to start the legal action from the beginning again, with the corrected name(s) spelled and all the lease parties included.

SERVE THE LEGAL NOTICE BY CONSTABLE OR SHERIFF

You are responsible for ensuring that the tenant receives the initial notice of termination of tenancy. Proof of service is prudent, and in some cases, may determine how far your case will proceed in court. The judge wants to be assured that the tenant was notified of your plan to evict, and was given adequate and timely notice for the tenant to cure the reason for the eviction.

I always send the notice by first-class mail, whether there is proof of service or not. People almost always read their mail even if they fail to acknowledge they received it. The point here is to make sure that the tenant knows you are processing legal papers for their eventual eviction. It is an extra measure of protection, especially if the letter comes back to you. If it does, do not open it. Save it as evidence for the judge of your attempt to inform the tenant if you end up in court. Consider this the lowest level of notification of an impending eviction.

Sending the notice by certified mail is a level up in notifying the tenant of your legal action. If you send a termination notice by certified mail, return receipt requested, the tenant could decide not to pick it up and sign for it. The post office will notify the tenant of the certified letter three times before it sends it back to you. If you get it back, do not open it. This is your evidence that your tenant failed to accept service.

If the tenant refuses to pick it up, you will lose time waiting for the notice to be returned to you. Meanwhile, the clock is still ticking. If you are filing for nonpayment of rent, by the time you receive confirmation from a certified letter that the tenant received the eviction notice, almost three weeks could have passed. If the tenant is dealing drugs or vandalizing your apartment, three weeks is a long time for more damage to be done.

If you use a constable, the service is faster. The constable's method of service is mandated under state law. He or she will deliver the notice directly to the tenant or leave it at the last known place of occupancy, namely, your tenant's apartment. The constable or sheriff should be familiar with the notification laws in the state as to how he or she must serve the tenant with eviction notices. After making service, he or she will return the original notice back to you with his or her certification of how and to whom the tenant notice was given and the date of service.

In some states, a sheriff must serve the notice to quit and all other notices if the rent due is more than a specific amount. Call your local courthouse and find out whether a constable or sheriff must serve your notice.

You can help your constable by telling him the best or most likely times the tenant will be home. In some states, service must be done during normal business hours. Some states will not allow a constable or sheriff to serve an eviction notice on a weekend, for example. Ask your constable or get a booklet from your state house on the eviction laws in your state for specific information.

RESERVE YOUR RIGHTS

Do not violate your own rights during the eviction process. Once you send the notice to quit, you have terminated the tenant's lease. Any money you receive from that point until the rent arrears is paid in full cannot be considered as rent. If you fail to put in writing that any money you receive from the tenant is "for occupancy only," and not for rent, you could reinstate the tenancy.

For example, when collecting funds during the legal process, always reserve your legal rights on the front or back of the check or money order. If you receive the rent in cash, give the tenant a receipt, and reserve your rights on both the tenant's copy and yours.

If you have implemented a rent increase and the tenant pays the original rent, you must reserve your rights on the back of the check and money order. If you do not, by accepting and depositing the old rent, you could send the message that you have decided against the rent increase for that tenant. Keep a copy of the note on the check or money order for your tenant's file.

The best way to reserve your rights is to write, "All legal rights reserved under eviction action"[17] on the money order or check.

If you give out receipts with a carbon, write this on the receipt, too.

Some states will not allow you to accept any monies at all once you send the initial eviction notice. I cannot emphasize enough the importance of checking with your local courthouse regarding the law in your state on your rights to receive rent money after you have notified the tenant with a Notice to Quit.

KEEP TRACK OF YOUR EVICTION TIMETABLES

Whether you have an attorney, you must keep track of your own lawsuit timetable. If you do not, you could lose by missing deadlines. A lawyer can miss a deadline date, and it is ultimately your role as the owner to follow your own cases and ensure they are being pursued with diligence and a sense of urgency.

If you have several evictions in line, use a checklist of all your tenants under eviction. Show when each notice was served and when the next step must be taken. Do this all the way to the actual move-out day and after the move-out, in accordance with Chapter 21.

WHAT TO DO WHEN THE TENANT WILL NOT COOPERATE

There are tenants who know the eviction process when it comes to repairs. They know what you must do and what they can do to stop you. Those tenants will not cooperate with you and your efforts to make repairs. You need to have a plan to deal with this problem.

- Notify the tenant in writing of when and what time you

or your contractor will be at the tenant's apartment to make repairs. You can tell the tenant in person also. A letter is documentation you can take to court to present as evidence that you gave good notice of service.

- The tenant should have at least 24 hours advance notice of the work. I always give 48 hours notice, to allow the tenant to make work and day care arrangements.

- Inform the tenant that you will charge a $25 fee for a missed appointment. Your time and that of your contractor is valuable, and the tenant needs to call you if he or she cannot make the appointed day and time.

- Have an answering machine, or better, a voice mail where the tenant can call you on a 24-hour basis to verify the appointment or ask for a reschedule. I do not charge for a rescheduled date.

- If the tenant is not home, leave your business card or have the contractor leave his card in the door.

- Send the tenant a letter indicating that either you or your contractor was at the apartment and the tenant was not available for the service. Ask him or her to call in the next 24 hours with a convenient date and time to make the repairs during business hours.

- If you are not already in court, take all of your letters and other documentation to the local housing department, the department of inspection services, or the department of health. Ask for their assistance in gaining entry to your own apartment. They can possibly run interference for you.

- Have an attorney send a letter for you, outlining what will happen if the tenant continues to hamper the landlord's efforts to maintain the property.

If all that fails, start the eviction. You will have more than enough evidence to prove your tenant is being obstructive toward your attempts at making repairs.

CHAPTER

16 WHEN & HOW TO HIRE AN ATTORNEY

Every homeowner, whether with tenants or not, should have a real estate or housing attorney. Housing laws have become more complicated over the years, forcing many homeowners to hire professional legal representation in eviction cases. Today, as always, "ignorance of the law is no excuse." If you do self-help in evicting your tenant and lose the case, you cannot say it was because you did not know what to do; that is the main reason for hiring a professional to conduct this type of legal business.

Having said this, if you have been doing fine evicting your tenants successfully, good for you. There are some experienced landlords who achieve proficient results doing their own lawsuits. There are other times and circumstances in which a good lawyer will save you the aggravation, time, and expense of trying your own eviction case.

WHEN TO HIRE AN ATTORNEY

Some cases are too important to lose. If your tenant is dealing drugs out of the apartment in a building filled with children, time is of the essence. If you do not know how to get that tenant or family out, this is no time to experiment with the legal system by trying to do it yourself. It is also not the time to use your family or friends for advice.

If you are unsure, hire an attorney. Do not try to save money where practicing the law is concerned. If you do it yourself and make errors, it could cost you three times the amount of the original back rent or triple damages paid to the tenant for violating his or her legal rights. Furthermore, if the tenant appeals the original court's opinion, he or she can take the eviction case to a higher court.

Your real estate attorney should be used for more than doing the title search and other legal paperwork when you first buy your house. Your lawyer should be the person who helps you get unreasonable tenants out of your house. Hire your attorney to get it done right.

Practice makes perfect. Many homeowners with experience have successfully evicted their tenants for nonpayment of rent or other lease violations. Perhaps they were or are a professional property manager. Many times, it works out fine for the owner.

However, if you get a sense that the case is not going well, or if the tenant has hired a lawyer, get your attorney to work with the tenant's attorney. Let the professionals haggle out the case in an efficient and legal manner.

If the tenant has hired a legal aid attorney, immediately hire your own lawyer. A legal aid attorney represents clients who are of low income and unable to hire an attorney to represent them at the standard attorney hourly rate. Legal aids fiercely pursue justice for their clients. The ability of a legal aid lawyer to file pages and pages of discovery and interrogatory documents is legendary.

Legal aid lawyers are known to be dedicated, relentless, and in most cases, excellent at their job. I have the utmost respect for their passion, extensive knowledge, experience, and diligence in defending their clients. For those reasons, I always have an attorney to represent my clients on an eviction case with a legal aid lawyer.

If you have a Section 8 tenant, you might want to hire an attorney. If your tenant files for bankruptcy while in your apartment, use an attorney. The bankruptcy laws are complicated, and, combined with a nonpayment of rent case, demand a person with thorough knowledge of both laws. Depending on the type of bankruptcy filed, your attorney will need to reserve your rent rights with the bankruptcy court. The attorney should also fight vigorously to separate your nonpayment of rent case from the bankruptcy case.

You never know what financial circumstances face a tenant. A tenant who files bankruptcy will increase the time spent on your eviction by several weeks. This is why, when your tenant fails to pay the rent on time, you should quickly send the notice to quit.

If you win your eviction case and the tenant files for an appeal of that decision, you might want to hire an attorney. Even though you have won your case, a tenant still has the right to appeal the judge's decision. Because the state laws regarding eviction appeals can be complicated, I recommend at least a consultation with an attorney, rather than winging it on your own.

Eviction Scenario - Tenant Wants More Money for His Work

Here is a good example of a situation in which I would hire an attorney without question.

You rented a two-bedroom apartment in your four-unit building to a single father, Eric Trouper (not his real name), who has a 6-year-old son. After a few rent increases, the current rent is a little steep for him to pay; you like the guy, so you work out a deal. The two of you have the understanding that he will take out the trash, keep the building clean, do some light painting, mow the lawn once a week, shovel snow as needed, and keep the place in order. In exchange, you will take $150 a month off the $950 per month rent, causing the tenant to pay $800 per month in rent.

This works well for two years. Now, the place looks so good, you implement a rent increase of $50 a month on everyone in the building, including Eric Trouper. Mr. Trouper informs you that he now wants $200 per month to keep the place clean. In other words, he does not want to pay the rent increase. He wants his rent to remain at $800 per month.

Mr. Trouper believes it has been his quality work on the property that has enabled you to raise the rent. Besides, the work to maintain the property is, in his opinion, now worth $200 per month. You have had *the benefit of using his services without a pay increase for two years. Your tenant strongly feels he is entitled to keep his rent the same amount.*

Unfortunately, this is something you did not anticipate. It is also something you are not willing to do. You do not believe that it takes $200 a month to keep the building clean. You also feel Mr. Trouper is being a little ungrateful because you did him a favor when you allowed him to have some of the rent cut off in the first place.

When Mr. Trouper fails to pay the rent increase, you send him an eviction notice for nonpayment of rent. In return, Mr. Trouper quits. He also applies for unemployment at the local Department of Labor. He tells officials that you have used his services as the building maintenance man for the past two years without paying unemployment insurance. The unemployment officials now want an explanation.

So does the IRS, who wants to know why you did not file the independent contractor form 1099 on Mr. Trouper for the past two years to show he received a financial benefit from the property. You figured that Mr. Trouper knew the cut in rent was considered income. He should have filed his taxes the right way. Neither do you have a lease on Mr. Trouper, nor did you enter into an independent contractor agreement with him.

In this situation, you should get legal advice from a good lawyer before you do anything else.

Where to Find an Attorney

You will be tempted to use the person you trust the most to do your eviction, but your eviction attorney should specialize in real estate law. A criminal or family court lawyer will know little about going to housing court. You also want a person who is well known in court by the judges and the clerks as being competent, fair, and honest in working eviction cases.

Here is where references or referrals from your friends, coworkers, and other homeowners can be helpful. Perhaps they had occasion to use a housing attorney successfully with a tenant.

Another way to find a good attorney is to call the local bar association.

Call a local property management company and ask whom it uses in court. It may use more than one lawyer in legal business with tenants. It is likely that whomever they recommend will be a good housing attorney who can handle your tenancy problems in an efficient, professional manner.

The Cost of an Attorney

You need to know how much your attorney will charge you for his or her work. You need to know the hourly rate before you hire him or her to conduct your case. Do not assume that the rate is one you can afford because you believe it will not be a difficult case to complete. This is a financial business decision that is critical to your real estate investment. You do not want to hire a high-powered attorney only to discover you cannot possibly pay the fee.

The attorney will give you his or her hourly rate. But the reality is, you will not be charged by the hour; you will be charged by the minute. In other words, each attorney has a minimum number of minutes charged. Some charge in ten-minute increments, some in 15-minute increments. You need to ask in what minimum increments you will be charged. Then, if you call your attorney to ask a "quick question," even if the answer takes him or her five minutes to respond to you, you will be charged the minimum incremental fee.

For example, let us say your attorney charges $110 per hour in 15-minute minimum increments. You call and talk for seven minutes about your case. You will be billed $27.50 for that short conversation. If you talk to your lawyer twice a week about your eviction case for ten to 15 minutes at a time, you could easily spend $220 or more in a month.

Inform your attorney that you want monthly, itemized invoices. This way, you will see everything your lawyer has done on your behalf, the amount of time spent for each action, and the cost for you to pay. You will also have the opportunity to keep current on your payments to your attorney or to review the invoice with him or her before it gets to a point where you will have a problem paying it.

When talking to your lawyer, you should remember that time is money; his or her time will cost you money. Be organized when you call. Write down the questions and points you want to know and make before the clock starts ticking on you. Be brief after you complete the amenities of a business call. You can swap anecdotes while the two of you are waiting for your eviction case to be called in court.

Expenses are not included in the hourly rate. Expenses could include the attorney's cost of parking for the court appearances, paying for the constable to serve the summons, telephone toll calls, postage, or court fees. You pay all expenses for the attorney to conduct your business, which is the eviction.

If you think these costs are expensive, figure out the financial cost of losing an eviction case and the cost of starting over from scratch. Compare the loss of rent, the complaints from your neighbors and other tenants, and the damage being done to your apartment the longer the tenant resides in the apartment. Compare this with having a professional get the eviction right the first time.

LET YOUR ATTORNEY DO THE JOB

You are paying an attorney by the hour to try your lawsuit. This person will represent you in court against the tenant or the tenant's lawyer. You hired a specialist in real estate law who will file the briefs, motions, and other paperwork necessary to successfully pursue the eviction case. If you hire an attorney for the eviction process, give your lawyer the respect, time, and opportunity to do the job. Do not hire a lawyer, then get upset if "nothing happens" for the first week.

Your lawyer will need time to read all the paperwork you provided and to prepare your case, especially if it is for cause. Never go behind your attorney's back and do something that might cause you to lose your case. Once you turn it over, turn it over completely. You need to trust your lawyer to do his or her job.

There are tenants who will try to "work things out" with you once you have hired legal counsel, but the time to work things out with you was before you were forced to hire an attorney. If the tenant had wanted to avoid a lawyer getting involved, he or she should have worked more closely with you to resolve the matter. Now, whatever the tenant needs or wants to say about the eviction should be said to your lawyer.

Using an attorney gives more formality to the eviction process. It lets the tenant know you are serious about collecting the rent or getting back the apartment. Whatever happened between you and the tenant induced you to believe that legal counsel was necessary. For the tenant, he or she knows that "game time" is over. It is much more difficult to manipulate, string along, or intimidate a lawyer than it is for a tenant to bully the homeowner.

STAY UPDATED

Staying updated does not mean that you call your attorney every other day, asking what is being done and when you will hear from him or her again. This also does not mean that you stop talking to your lawyer until he or she tells you it is time to go to court. You should expect and receive copies of all correspondence and whatever is filed in court.

A good attorney will call you on a regular basis and tell you what is going on from week to week. You can also call periodically for quick, verbal progress reports, but you pay for each conversation you have with your attorney.

17

WHAT TO DO
BEFORE YOU
GO TO COURT

D ecide from the beginning what is most important to you — the money or the apartment. You might have to decide which you want more before a judge, who could offer you one option or the other but not both. Sometimes, you can have both, if you prove your case to the judge's satisfaction. Still, be prepared to get the eviction notice but no rent arrears judgment.

Do not violate your tenant's rights, access to the building or the apartment, or their privacy during the eviction process. This means you should not change the locks to the apartment or the front entry door, call the tenant, or try to get him or her to move out before the court date. If you want to try to settle out of court, see Chapter 19 for more on this subject.

DECIDE WHICH COURT WILL TRY YOUR CASE

You will have to try your eviction case in the jurisdiction where the property is located. If you live in Ohio, and the property is located in Illinois, you will have to file your case in Illinois.

There is more than one courthouse where you can take your

eviction case. Ask your attorney about the best one for your situation. Civil court will handle your case strictly by the facts. Housing court will take other matters, such as the condition of the apartment, into consideration.

If your city has housing court, take your eviction case there. In Massachusetts, the cost of filing a civil eviction case is almost twice the cost of filing in housing court. This is one way to get every landlord to file in housing court first.

If your city or town does not have housing court, civil court will be your only option. Either way, your preparation should be the same. You might need more evidence in housing court than civil court.

You should know that if you file a civil eviction in a city with housing court, the tenant has the option of having the case transferred to housing court. This will delay your eviction until the transfer paperwork and new trial date is decided. This is why most housing managers and savvy homeowners go straight to housing court with their eviction cases. It saves time.

PREPARE YOUR CASE IN ADVANCE

Talk to your attorney about the case. Decide what your "bottom line" is in the case. That is, what is the most compromise you are willing to accept, and what will you absolutely not agree to? If the tenant asks for an additional month to move out, will that be all right with you? If he or she needs three months to move out, will you agree to that?

Decide on whether you will agree to mediation. This is where the judge asks a court clerk to try to work things out between the landlord and the tenant. If it cannot, and either party still wants to go before the judge, then it can still happen. If agreement is made with the help of the clerk, then that agreement is written up for the judge's review and approval.

You might be in conflict with your tenant about the lack of repairs in the apartment; your nonpayment of rent case could be based on the completion of specific repair work. If it is legal in your state, instruct your attorney to ask the court to put the tenant's rent in escrow, with the tenant's attorney, or even your own attorney, while repairs are being completed. When the work is finished, you want your rent turned over to you.

GATHER AND REVIEW YOUR EVIDENCE

Regardless of whether you use an attorney, it is your responsibility to prove your case. This means that concrete, written evidence or proof must be presented to a judge. Put all your evidence in a folder, and do not forget to bring it all to court. Many cases are lost because the owner fails to bring his documentation and evidence to court. Your letters of termination, and any other warning letters you sent to the tenant to prove your case, are crucial pieces of evidence. Do not forget to bring copies of letters the tenant sent to you.

A copy of the lease is essential to bring to court. It confirms what the tenant violated and what prompted you to take action. Keep the original in the tenant folder, and provide the judge with a copy. Also bring any lease addendum and any rules or policies you have implemented on your tenants.

The judge does not want to hear he-said-she-said testimony. The judge wants to see written, audio, or visual evidence to back up your case. If your tenant beat you up, bring the ripped shirt as evidence to court. If your clothes got bloodied, do not try to wash it off; bring it just as it was damaged during the altercation. If you have the fistfight on videotape, bring that also. If you filed a police report, bring it to court. If you did not file a police report after all the above, you better have a good reason to give to the judge.

Bring a copy of every police report made on the apartment. You cannot just say to the judge that the police have been to the tenant's apartment seven times. You must produce seven police reports as evidence. Your police department can provide you with either individual police reports or a list of all visits to the street address for each month in question. If you have to pay for the reports, pay it. This is your day in court. You must have all the evidence to prove your case.

Depending on the nature of your case, whether for nonpayment of rent or the termination of the lease for cause, you need to set up and follow a checklist to make sure you bring all your evidence with you to court. You do not want to be in the position of losing your case because of a missing piece of evidence. Here is an example of what your court appearance checklist should include:

- The original lease, as signed by both you and the tenant

- The original of any lease addendum, addition, or changes to the lease

- The original copy of all Section 8 lease and other paperwork, if applicable

- The original apartment inspection report, as signed by

both you and the tenant, proving the original condition of the apartment before the tenant moved in

- Any subsequent apartment inspections signed by you and the tenant showing the changed condition of the apartment since the tenant moved in

- A copy of any rules, policies, or procedures that the tenant violated, with the tenant signature on the original copy or proof that the tenant received a copy

- The original nonpayment of rent notice or termination letter to the tenant

- Proof that the above notice of termination document was served to the tenant and proof that the tenant received it. If the tenant did not pick up the certified letter, do not open it. Bring the unopened envelope to court.

- Copies of warning letters sent to the tenant, in chronological order

- Copies of letters you sent asking the tenant to pay the rent, in chronological order

- Any and all original e-mails sent to you by the tenant and those you sent to the tenant, in chronological order

- Text messages or voice mail audio tape of negative conversations with or from the tenant

- The original or copy of any signed rent payment agreement between you and the tenant

- Copies of incident reports made on the tenant or the building involving the tenant under eviction (see Appendix)

- Notarized witness statements supporting your case, if the person cannot go to court with you

- A copy of every police report filed on the tenant, the apartment, or the building

- Copies of repair bills paid for the apartment and/or building over the past year. The bills you bring should be those that were necessary because of the tenant.

- Copies of any letters you sent asking the tenant to pay for damages to the apartment or building

- Copies of all rent payment checks received from the tenant during the time you notified the tenant of the legal case for nonpayment of rent. This includes copies of all Section 8 checks received, if applicable. Each copied check or money order should be stamped "For use and occupancy only. All legal rights reserved." on the front or back, from the time you first sent the notice to quit. If you received cash, bring your rent receipt book. If you use a computer program to post rent posted and received, bring a copy of the tenant's rent report.

- If you sent any letter or notice by return receipt request, bring that with you to court as proof that the letter was either picked up by the tenant or returned to you undelivered.

Your paperwork should be in chronological order by date and category. All police reports should be paper-clipped together, letters from the tenant paper-clipped together, and so on. You cannot fumble around looking for information when the judge asks for a special document. Put your papers in order in a file folder, or have a file folder for each document set.

This may seem like too much information to bring to court, but you never know what the judge is going to ask you to produce as evidence. You do not want to be in a position where you lose a case because you failed to bring a piece of evidence the judge needed to make a good decision.

Your case will, most often, be tried and decided on the day you go into court. If you have to say, "I have it at home, Your Honor," or "I forgot to bring it with me," you might not look good in the judge's eyes. The judge might consider your failure to bring every piece of possible evidence to prove your case to court as a way to favor the tenant's testimony. You and your attorney are equally responsible for proving your case. Written documentation can rarely go wrong.

If you are using an attorney, he will ask for all your written or picture evidence to present your case in court. Always make a copy of whatever you send to your lawyer. Evidence lost in the mail, such as an income tax return, is evidence possibly gone forever without a backup copy at home.

APARTMENT INSPECTION REPORTS

You should have conducted a written apartment inspection before you gave out the keys to your apartment. You and the tenant should have signed this document, agreeing on the condition of the apartment before the tenant moved in. A year or six months later, you should have conducted a new written apartment inspection. This inspection would show any damages, alterations, or additions to your apartment since the original move-in date.

If you are evicting for damages to the apartment, vandalism, serious harm done to the unit, or any significant changes to the apartment, you might need to show what condition the apartment was in before the damage was done. Otherwise, you leave the decision up to the judge as to what the tenant did or did not do to the unit.

WITNESS TESTIMONY

A witness to any crime or incident that occurred on your property is always a strong factor in your favor. If you can get a witness to go to court with you and testify to some of the atrocities you want the judge to hear, bring the person(s). A witness is always good for telling what happened on a given date and time that would cause you to file for an eviction.

On the other hand, do not expect a witness to volunteer to go to court on your behalf. Even if a witness is one of your tenants, even if that tenant was the one complaining about the other tenant, do not expect his or her cooperation.

In many cases, the tenant might not want to be a witness for fear of being labeled a "snitch." Tenants who go to court to witness against another tenant in the building or neighborhood could be retaliated against after the case is over. This is a real situation for your witness and should be raised while meeting to ask for cooperation in your legal case.

Be careful whom you use for your witness. For example, you do not want to use a drug user to testify against a tenant you suspect of dealing drugs. You also should not use a tenant as a witness whom you think you might have to evict later on. Never pay a tenant to snitch on another tenant. It could taint your case, as the tenant could be accused of saying whatever you paid her to say, even if it is the truth.

I have tried hard during my career not to use a tenant as a witness. It puts them in a sticky situation. If your tenant lives in the same building with the tenant you are trying to evict, getting that person as a witness will be next to impossible. The tenant has to think about what could happen to him or her if you lose the case. If he or she has testified against the next-door neighbor and you lose the case, the tenant might confront that person about the testimony.

There are some tenants who will testify, depending upon the nature of the case. Consider the witnesses' time. If he or she will miss a day from work in order to appear in court or if he or she appears reluctant when you ask for the appearance, you might have to subpoena the witness to ensure he or she shows up in court and testifies.

A subpoena is a legal document issued by the court requiring the witness to appear in person at a certain place, date, and time to testify about a case. Subpoenas may be delivered in person by a police officer or any other person at least 18 years old and not a party to the lawsuit. If you or your lawyer does this, that person might end up a hostile witness. Consider how vital that person's testimony is to your case before taking subpoena action.

Depending upon the seriousness of the problem, some witnesses will not take a day off to go to court and lose a day's pay. They might not be willing to go and be paid the standard jury pay. You should then ask for a witness statement. Ask the witness to write a notarized letter outlining the complaint, and get it at least a week before the trial date. If you can get a witness to put something in writing, get it as soon as possible after the offer. Offer to pay for the notary, which is a legal property expense.

There are circumstances where the police department, drug enforcement unit staff, or other pertinent agency staff will testify for you on behalf of the city. Talk to your authority contact people and ask if they will testify. You could be pleasantly surprised by their answer.

POLICE REPORTS

If your tenant has been giving loud parties, conducting illegal activities at the apartment, or just plain been a nuisance, there might be a report somewhere at police headquarters. You can get a copy of all the police reports made on the street where the tenant lives.

This is one of the best pieces of legal documentation you can bring to present your eviction case. Your case is stronger when you can show the judge a series of police reports of activities at your tenant's apartment.

You might be reluctant to call the police on your tenant when he or she is living right above your apartment. The tenant cannot help but know or figure out that it is you calling the police on them all the time. Expect the tenant to confront you at some point.

Do not be intimidated by a tenant confrontation. Your tenant is anxious about you trying to move him out of the apartment. Stay calm; if you speak to the tenant with respect and professionalism, the tenant might do the same. If you lose control and start raising your voice, the tenant has you where he wants you.

Ask to discuss the matter further at another time if you feel yourself getting angry and out of control. Assure him that you will allow him another opportunity to talk about the problem the next day, and mean it. Speak to him and give him the opportunity to correct the problem before the eviction train starts to move out of the station.

PHOTOGRAPHS

If you are evicting because of excessive damages and/or abuse of the apartment, a picture can speak a thousand words for you. After you notify your tenant that you will be entering the apartment for an inspection, you have the right to take pictures of the apartment condition. A picture of the atrocities with the date is an excellent way to prove your case for other than nonpayment of rent (See Chapter 6).

As always, take a newspaper with you with the date you are doing the apartment inspection. Put the newspaper in front of every item you consider damage, and take a picture with the newspaper date visible.

Similarly, if you made repairs yourself, you should take a picture of the completed work, again with the newspaper showing the date the repair was made. If something happens to the repair afterward, you can show that the work was completed in a proper manner on the date in question. If the tenant refuses to sign your work order form, the picture can be used as evidence of satisfactory completion of work.

RECEIPTS AND CANCELED CHECKS

If your case is for nonpayment of rent, bring your rent receipt book with you. It should document all the payments you received from the tenant, when, and how much. You should have recorded any cash payments made on this receipt book.

If you put your rental income information on a computer program, such as QuickBooks Pro, you should take a copy of the financial reports on your tenant.

If your case is for nonpayment of rent pending the completion of repairs, you should prepare to bring all your paid vendor receipts with you. If repairs were made by a handyman, have the tenant sign off on a repair work order that the work was done to his or her satisfaction.

If you did not have a signed contract with a vendor, bring the original canceled checks to court. This will prove your out-of-pocket damages and repairs made in the tenant's apartment or the building.

DOCUMENT CONTINUED VIOLATIONS

Your tenant might not stop his or her behavior just because you sent an eviction notice. If anything, the behavior might get worse, because now the tenant feels he or she has little to lose. The tenant might also be angry about having to make a court appearance and miss work.

Your job is to document any behavior similar to the behavior that caused you to file for eviction. Second, if the tenant begins any new or different negative behavior, that behavior should be documented as well. A letter sent to the tenant informing him or her that this new negative behavior has been noted, and that a memo has been added to the tenant's file folder, is a good idea. Make sure your attorney gets a copy of the letters.

Expect the tenant to get angry over all the letters, notices, and other paperwork sent to his or her home. Even expect a visit from the tenant protesting the correspondence and stating that you are harassing the household. Remain calm. Explain to the tenant that you are merely documenting your legal case and that if the negative behavior were to change, you would not have to document it for your court appearance.

Incident reports after sending the eviction notice are good proof to the judge that the tenant is either unwilling or unable to change his or her behavior or those of family and visitors. Stay vigilant on your case until it is heard in court.

BE PREPARED FOR AN OFFER

You should be prepared for almost anything before you go to court. A tenant or his attorney might make an offer to pay the entire rent, arrange a rent payment plan, or leave the apartment by a specific date before the court date. Some tenants do not want an eviction case on their record. Others might have been stalling for time until they could find another apartment. In any event, you should have some idea of what outcome you want from the tenant. A payment plan is not the same as a writ of possession. Any agreement made should be executed in court. The mutual agreements should be presented before the judge as without hesitation or coercion.

18 YOUR COURT APPEARANCE

If this is your first time in court, chances are, it will not be your last time going to court while you own the property. Maybe, as a seasoned homeowner, you have been to court many times — so many times that the court clerks and judge know you by name.

Regardless of your court experience, the proper professional respect and attitude should be maintained while in court. This is not the place to bring a newspaper, a book, your cell phone, or MP3 player. You are not in court to be entertained. You have already spent or lost thousands of dollars getting to this point in court. Do not blow it by behaving improperly.

Bring all your paperwork, pictures, vendor receipts, canceled checks, letters, e-mails, and other documents written between you and the tenant with you to court. Do not leave behind anything associated with the tenant. Do not be in the position of having the judge ask you to present a document that you do not have because you did not think it was important. Everything in writing is important until the case is over. Bring the tenant's entire file folder with you, organized by date.

Wear Appropriate Clothes to Court

A courthouse is a place of business, and your personal appearance is important. Do not disrespect the court, the judge, or your case by arriving dressed as though you are planning to go to the beach afterward. No one says you have to wear a suit and tie to court. Wearing shorts and open-toed sandals, however, shows that you have a casual attitude about your court appearance. If you want the judge to take your case seriously, wear serious clothing.

Show Up on Time

The court has many cases to hear. Therefore, court starts on time. Do not arrive late to court. Your case could come and go before you get off the bus or park your car in the parking lot. If you need to use the restroom, do it before court begins. You want to be sitting in the courtroom when court starts. The clerks will sometimes call names out quickly when the time to start court begins.

You have spent money and taken time to prepare for this day. Do not spoil it by showing up late. Get to court at least 45 minutes before the specified time. If you appear late for your own case and miss "the call," your eviction case, in most states, will be dismissed for your failure to appear to prosecute.

Find Your Case and Go to Mediation

When you get to court, go immediately to the civil clerk's office to find your case and the room number where your case will be heard. There is often a bulletin board where you can find your case on a sheet or several sheets of paper. It tells in which order the cases will be heard.

The person filing the eviction case is called the plaintiff. The person against whom the eviction is filed (your tenant) is called the defendant. If you have filed your case *pro se*, this will be added to your name as the plaintiff. *Pro se* means that you are representing yourself in court without the benefit of an attorney.

Go immediately to the room where your case will be heard. The clerk of the court will be at the front of the court, going through the cases. You can either go over to the clerk to let him or her know that you are in the courtroom or take a seat and wait for your case to be heard.

When there are several hundred cases to be heard, in large city courts, you may be asked if you wish to go to mediation. Sometimes you are required to go to mediation before the judge will hear your case. Mediation is where both you and the tenant, with one of the court clerks, go to see if you can work things out. Both you and the tenant must agree to go to mediation. If either one refuses, the clerk will keep you on the docket to be heard by the judge.

The benefit of going to mediation is that you get to be heard sooner rather than later. The clerk still has to have the judge sign off on any written agreement made between the two parties, but, you have the opportunity to have your case heard in an area where just the three of you are sitting. Your case does not get heard before the entire courtroom of people waiting for their own cases. If the two of you and the clerk cannot work things out, the judge can still hear your case.

STAY IN THE COURTROOM

Staying in the courtroom seems obvious, yet I have seen more eviction cases dismissed because the landlord or property manager has left. Once court begins, the clerk calls all the names of the people who are on the court docket for the day. Both the plaintiff's and the defendant's names will be called. The clerk wants to make sure everyone is there before he or she calls in the judge.

While you are outside having a quick cigarette, your case could be called. Sometimes the court clerk will go out in the hallway and call the name of the next case. Even then, there could be so much noise in the hallway that you could miss hearing your name.

Stay in the courtroom until your case number comes up. You have spent your time and money preparing your case. You want and need to explain your case to the judge, and you hope for a decision made in your favor. Do not lose it all by leaving the courtroom and missing your call.

You might have to wait extra time if the tenant needs or has asked for a translator in his or her native language. The court should have translators available for such situations. However, if the language is unusual for the court in your jurisdiction, you may have to wait until a translator can be found and sent to translate your case. The court clerk will let you know if that happens.

When you enter the courtroom, you will be required to take a seat. Standing is frowned upon, unless all the available seats are taken. The clerk will ask you to be seated until your case is called. You are also restricted from reading a newspaper or book, using your phone or MP3 player, chewing gum (a big court offense), or from bringing any food or drink into the courtroom.

Above all else, there is no talking in the courtroom. You might not even be allowed to whisper to your attorney. All attention is to be focused on the court proceedings. I have seen many people asked to leave the courtroom for whispering to someone else while court is in session. The judge remembers those people asked to leave when they come up before him or her for their case.

When the judge enters the room, the clerk will shout, "All rise. Court is in session," and everyone must stand up. When the judge has taken his or her seat, then the courtroom people may sit also. This is out of respect for the judge, the court setting, the significance of the court system, and respect for the law. If you remain sitting and you show no signs of infirmity, you could be asked to leave the courtroom until your case is called.

STAY LATE

When your case is called, both parties have to indicate they are in the courtroom. The court clerk may call out all the cases to get an idea of which cases are ready, want to be rescheduled, or those cases that will be given a default judgment. If at first the court clerk calls both plaintiff and defendant and you are the only one who answers, the clerk may hold your case for "second call." After the second call is completed, a default judgment is given to the party who shows up for the court appearance.

There are tenants who have been through the eviction process before who might show up after they think the case is over and you have already left the court for the day. If you have left court and the tenant can give a court clerk a good excuse why he or she was late, he or she can ask for the case to be rescheduled. If allowed, this could give the tenant an extra ten days before the 213 case is heard in court again. You will be required to show up on the rescheduled date.

To avoid this happening, after the case is called for the second time, always stay in court for at least an hour. This way, if or when the tenant appears late, you are still available, and you or your attorney can ask the court to put the case back on for a hearing.

Of course, waiting around is extra time and money you have to pay your attorney, but it is cheaper than having to pay for that day and then pay again for another day in court. It is also valuable time if you stay in the courtroom and listen to other eviction cases being heard. You will get a sense of the kind of cases that are tried and decided, how owners and attorneys present their cases, and how the judge considers evidence and testimony in making his or her decisions.

If you receive a default judgment, your time in court is over. The eviction has been granted because the tenant failed to defend against the case. Go back to the court clerk's office to see if you have to file any additional paperwork before you go home.

Your day in court could take as little as two hours or as long as eight hours. If you are successful, it is worth the wait.

Wait Your Turn to Talk

Your court appearance is not your chance to say whatever you want to say. This is not the place where you and the tenant get to talk over one another. No matter what you see on television, the rule for court behavior is courtesy and respect. Wait until the judge asks you to speak before you give your testimony. Be quiet when he or she tells you to be quiet.

If you have an attorney, he or she will do all your talking for you. A good attorney will prepare you for your court appearance. He or she will discuss the questions you will be asked by him or her, by the tenant's attorney, or by the judge.

WATCH WHAT YOU SAY

When you give evidence or testimony, the court clerk is recording you, making an audio transcript of the case. The transcript of the court proceedings is typed up and available for review (at a price) by either party if there is an appeal, word for word. Therefore, you want to watch what you say in court and how you say it. For example, sarcasm might sound cute in court, but it looks bad on paper.

If you hear something your tenant says that makes you angry, do not scream or swear. Do not mumble under your breath. Keep your composure at all times. The judge, clerk, and everyone associated with the court system will remember you for your behavior.

Keep your anger under control. If you misbehave or shout too many times, the judge could hold your behavior in contempt. If you have an attorney, sometimes the judge will order you out of the courtroom and allow your attorney to represent you alone. You do not want this to happen just because you could not keep your mouth closed during your case.

The judge might ask you questions that you might not want to answer. If, for example, she wants to know what you do for a

215

living and you feel that question is not relevant to the eviction case, you have the right to refuse to answer. At the same time, the judge will take your refusal to answer questions she might feel are relevant into consideration while deciding the case.

Do not interrupt the judge when he or she speaks. If you are speaking, you are not listening to what the judge has to say. Do not attempt to battle with the judge over how the case is going. The judge may decide that you are a disrespectful person if you keep trying to talk at the same time as he or she is speaking.

If you think you will not be able to behave yourself in court, you should have an attorney speak for you. He or she will be objective and non-emotional with the judge, making points and stating facts as opposed to quoting opinions or speaking emotionally about the tenant.

The judge will try to be lenient with you for a while. He or she understands that landlord/tenant cases tend to be emotional times for both parties. Still, the proper decorum should be upheld. For example, it does not make you look classy if you call your tenant names while giving testimony. Sarcasm will get you only so far as well. Constantly interrupting your tenant while he or she is talking is not permissible. It would go a long way for you to be as professional as possible during your trial.

BE PREPARED

This is your only day in court for this case. You are expected to present a factual case before a judge, with written and/or photo evidence to back up every claim you make about your tenant. If you say your tenant is disruptive to the property, you should have police reports, letters you sent to the tenant, and any other documentation to defend that accusation. If you have much information to present, make sure it is organized by date.

Do not think you will have only one eviction case in the lifetime of your property. A housing court judge has a good memory for regulars. Respect the judge's time with a professional presentation, and you will be remembered. Go to court and tie up the judge's time by filtering through your envelopes full of paper, and you will also make an impression.

If you have witnesses, they should sit with you in court. They should not sit with, nor talk to, your tenant under eviction. This is not a social situation. It is administrative combat. Find out when your witnesses plan to arrive in court. Better, inform them when they should arrive in court, at least 45 minutes before court begins. Then you can review their testimony before court begins.

Expect the tenant to be prepared as well, with evidence of his or her own, if not a rebuttal to your claims of nonpayment of rent or lease violations. Also expect your tenant to say almost anything to form an attack. After all, he or she is fighting to stay in the apartment.

You may hear testimony from your tenant that is totally incorrect in fact or in your opinion. This is not the time to yell out, "She's lying, Your Honor." That happens only on television. It will not get you points from the judge. You should be prepared to have a written rebuttal to everything the tenant says. Write down what your tenant said, and when asked, present your rebuttal. Refer to your notes when you give your response to stay in control of your presentation. Better yet, write down and give your comments to your attorney, if you have one with you.

After hearing both parties, the judge may tell you he or she is taking the case "under advisement." This is another way for the judge to say he or she does not want to embarrass the losing party with everyone in the courtroom. The judge will issue his or her final verdict through the mail. You can also call the court toward the end of the day with your case number. Representatives might be willing to tell you over the phone, if the judge has decided by then.

Require a Court Payment Plan

Sometimes the tenant will come to court with a partial rent payment. Then, the tenant will ask you to continue the case to another date to give him or her time to pay the remainder of the rent. Do not accept it. Tell the tenant that you prefer to go before the judge. He or she can present the monies to the judge as a partial payment.

You also have the option of going to a housing mediator and asking to have a payment plan written for you with both parties in agreement. The mediator will then present the agreement to the judge. He will ask both of you whether the agreement was done of your own free will and without duress.

After going through the court process, a tenant is less likely to violate a court-ordered rent payment plan than one you wrote. If the tenant fails to comply, you can go back to court and file a motion for a writ of possession. In some states, if a court-ordered rent payment plan is violated, the writ is issued immediately upon request.

HOW YOUR CASE MAY BE DECIDED

Based on the evidence, the judge in most cases will decide the case right then and there in court. Especially in nonpayment of rent cases, unless there are extenuating circumstances, the judge may grant the eviction to the homeowner.

If the tenant says he or she did not pay the rent because of code violations, the judge has the option of holding off on deciding an eviction case pending an inspection report. The inspection is to determine the condition and habitability of the apartment and the building. The judge might want to get a report from his or her court staff regarding the condition of the unit, if code violations are the reason for nonpayment of rent by the tenant.

If code violations are found, the landlord might not receive permission to evict from the judge until the violations have been addressed. Once the repairs have been considered corrected by the housing inspector, you will receive a notice to return to court and get a judgment based on the results.

After your case has been heard and decided in your favor, again, leave the tenant alone. Say as little as possible. I have seen landlords do a dance after winning a case. I have seen landlords taunt the tenant in court about winning the case. It will not win you points with the judge or the court clerks. You might have to see these court employees again. Be a gracious winner.

There is some paperwork to be filled out. If you made an

agreement in court, you might have to stay until the clerk writes it up. You will be asked to move into a room until your name is called. You and the tenant will be asked whether you both consent to the written agreement.

WHAT HAPPENS WITH THE EVICTION NOTICE

If you win your case, depending on your state eviction laws, the notice to evict will be mailed to you in three to ten days. Once you receive it, you will have a specific amount of time to use it or lose it. You do not have to use it immediately after you receive it, but you have to use it by the expiration date. Failing that, you will have to start the eviction all over again. Once used, the original notice goes back to the housing court for the record by the constable or sheriff who observed or completed the eviction.

RENT ESCROW LAW

There are landlords who do not give the proper attention to their properties. When that happens, the tenant has the right either to stop paying the rent or withhold a certain amount of the rent until the repairs are made up to code.

Rent escrow is one of the best ways that both the landlord and the tenant can win in eviction court. Rent escrow applies if the tenant has been withholding rent because of the lack of repairs and maintenance of the property. For example, since October 1997 New York City has had a rent escrow law. It mandates a means to account for tenant responsibility for their failure to pay rent during the eviction process.

EVICTION TIP

The tenant may be required to deposit money in the form of a check or money order, before the eviction case is over, if the tenant asks for two adjournments (time for a new court date) or, if the case has been in the court for 30 days. If either of these two things happen, the landlord or his attorney can ask the judge to order the tenant to deposit money with the court, a financial institution, or an attorney.

Before the tenant is ordered to deposit money, he or she will be sent to a rent deposit courtroom. The judge may hold a hearing to determine whether the tenant has to make the deposit and what amount should be deposited. The tenant may not be asked to make a rent deposit based on matters of income, errors in court documents, apartment condition, or jurisdiction.

Failure to make the rent deposit as instructed will allow the landlord to ask for an immediate judgment without a trial, or the judge can order an immediate trial.

Adapted from New York City-Wide Task Force on Housing Court Fact Sheet, (**www.cwtfhc.org**)

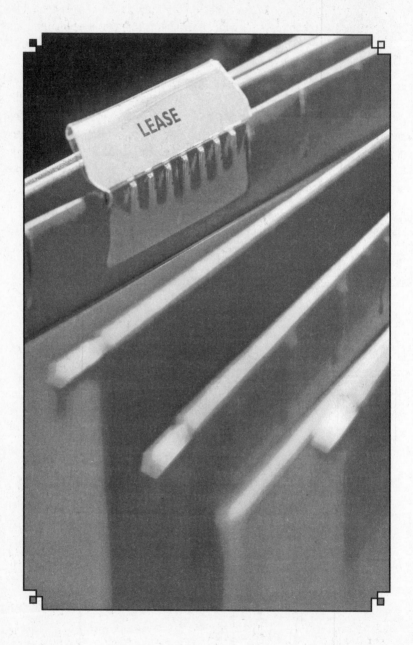

19 SETTLING OUT OF COURT

Your eviction case is going on too long. It is taking up more of your time and energy than you anticipated when you first initiated it. A lengthy eviction happens with cases that do not have rent as an issue. If you are evicting a tenant for excessive damage or illegal activities, or if you have a tenant who is fighting back to prevent eviction, you might at some point just want to put the entire situation behind you as quickly as possible.

The alternative to going to court is having a mutual and voluntary agreement between you and the tenant. Both parties often agree, in consideration of a mutual benefit, that the tenant will move out before or after going to court. The primary goal of settling out of court is to get the tenant to move out on his or her own without going through a prolonged court case. Essentially, the tenant gets to leave without an eviction record. He or she gets to live another day with another landlord, likely an unwitting one.

There are landlords who will tell you that you can "pay off" a tenant to move out by forgiving the rent arrears and/or by offering the tenant the security deposit back and sometimes a sum of money on top of all that. This is done in an attempt at avoiding going through the legal eviction process. Sometimes it works; sometimes it does not. There are times and opportunities to use this tactic as a way for everyone to win.

SETTLEMENT OPTIONS

Decide how desperate you are to get the tenant out of your building. How tight is your case? Do you think you might lose if you go to court? Are you afraid you might make a mistake and have to start the process all over? Here are some advantages of settling out of court:

- You avoid taking time out from work for costly court time.

- Your legal fees are avoided.

- You might end up paying less than you would if you went ahead with the eviction.

- Further damage to your apartment is prevented.

- You can stipulate that once the tenant and family move out of the apartment, they are never to return to the building, nor apply to any other property you own or manage.

- Your neighbors do not care how you get rid of your problem tenant, as long as it is fast.

- The faster you get the bad tenant out, the faster you can get a good tenant moved in.

Settling out of court should never be an act of desperation.

If done at all, it should be a well-calculated risk and a precise negotiation. The advantage to the tenant is, by moving out before the case gets to court, he or she will avoid having an eviction record on file. None of your eviction work will be a matter of public record. Here are some settlement options:

- Pay the tenant a sum of money to move out and get another apartment. It should be enough to pay for the rent and security deposit.

- Give the tenant a specific amount of time to move out. Rent will be free for that time period so the tenant can save to move out.

- If the tenant has filed for bankruptcy, he or she might be agreeable to an offer of cash for a specific move-out date.

WHAT HAPPENS WHEN YOU SETTLE OUT OF COURT?

If you have a case where the tenant has vandalized or destroyed property, cost you much in lost rent, repairs, reputation, and aggravation, you should want the case to be heard in open court where other landlords and rental managers are present. Real estate professionals like to jot down the name(s) of those tenants who might end up in their laps in the future. There is real merit in having your problem(s) with the tenant heard and published by the judge.

Having said that, if you decide to settle out of court, here is what could happen and what the tenant may ask:

- The tenant may ask for money you do not currently have or for more than you can afford.

- The tenant may ask that you never give a negative landlord reference report on her.

- The tenant could require that you do not file a negative credit report on her.

- The tenant will not have an eviction record, because you both decided not to go to court.

- You will not tell Section 8 you were planning to file a drug eviction.

- You are sending the tenant out to possibly do the same thing to another landlord.

- The tenant may ask for an extended time to stay in the apartment rent free so that she can save up for another apartment.

- The tenant may require that you pay her moving costs, in addition to everything else.

- If the tenant senses you want or need him or her gone as soon as possible, the stakes will go higher.

- Your settlement will be perceived as you having "deep pockets," thereby encouraging more of these types of move-outs.

The process of settling out of court should be a mutual and voluntary agreement. You cannot bully a tenant into moving out on his or her own. Both parties still have the right to have a day in court; negotiations will entail compromise from both sides.

All negotiations should be worked out in writing and included in the agreement. Avoid verbal agreements. If anything goes wrong, you will need a document proving what the two of you agreed to. A verbal agreement gone wrong, causing you to continue the eviction case, will be open to interpretation in court.

Before you say one word to the tenant about offering a settlement, think carefully about your limitations. Decide the maximum amount you are willing to pay for the tenant to move out. Start your discussion with the tenant by offering less than the amount you are willing to pay. This will give you some room for negotiation.

When you meet with the tenant, wear your best poker face. This is a business negation. While speaking with the tenant or while signing the agreement, never show whether you are angry or happy about the outcome.

20 EVICTION RECEIVED – PREPARE FOR THE MOVE-OUT DAY

From the time you first serve the notice to quit to when you receive the eviction notice could take from three weeks to six months. From the time you went to court to when you receive the eviction notice should be about ten days. This is if the tenant does not appeal the eviction judgment.

You must have the legal document from the court in your hand before you can evict the tenant. Do not jump the gun and try to evict the tenant before you receive the official court notification. Do not change the locks to the apartment or do anything else to the tenant's unit. In most cases, if an attorney represented you, he or she will receive the eviction notice and will contact you for further instructions as to when you want it served on the tenant.

You will have to give the tenant advance notice that you intend to evict. In some states, the notice is three days, but this may vary. The point is that the tenant must be notified of the exact date he or she will be removed from the property. A constable or sheriff must serve the eviction notice.

You need to be advised by your constable when you can begin the eviction. In most states, the eviction must be completed during business hours and on a business day. This prevents a homeowner from arriving at the tenant's apartment at seven o'clock in the morning, preventing him or her from going to court for a stay of the eviction.

Changed Your Mind About The Tenant?

If the judge gives you judgment on your tenant for nonpayment of rent, the tenant might pay the full amount due plus the court costs, before the three or ten-day waiting period is over. There might be many changes since you began the eviction process for nonpayment of rent. Perhaps the tenant has a new job and now will have the money to pay.

At the beginning of this book, we discussed what outcome you wanted from the eviction process. Go to Chapter 13, and review your decision making process.

There are several things to consider. Do you think this situation was unusual, or do you think it will happen again if you allow the tenant to stay? Was this the first time you have had to take legal action on this tenant? How long has the tenant been living there? How long will the tenant keep the new job? You are entitled to change your mind. Just make sure it is for the right business reasons.

Is the Tenant Already Gone?

When you receive the notice to evict, the tenant receives a similar notice that you have won the eviction. The tenant might start packing to be out by the time you receive the document. Some tenants go into denial, hoping that they will be able to come up with the rent money in full. Others will try to move so you cannot use the eviction notice on them. They are aware that an eviction notice filed with the court will follow them for a long time.

If you give the tenant the required three-day notice to move, chances are, that is not enough time to move on their own. It is not even enough time to find another apartment and have the first month's rent and security deposit. If you are evicting the tenant for nonpayment of rent, finding another apartment in three days, or even ten days, will be almost impossible.

However, it does happen that the tenant is able to move out at some point during the ten-day waiting period and the three-day notification period. You might see the tenant move out, or perhaps another tenant or neighbor will inform you of the move-out.

You have two choices. You can consider the apartment as abandoned, see if everything is gone, and recover the unit. Or you can have the constable serve the eviction notice anyway and enter the apartment in accordance with the court order.

If the constable serves the notice, even if the apartment is abandoned, it will be considered a legal eviction. The notice must go back to the court as served, and the tenant will have an eviction record.

FIND AND HIRE A CONSTABLE OR SHERIFF

Go back to your state eviction laws. Some states require that either a constable or sheriff evict a tenant, based on how much money the tenant owes. Go over the execution notice with your constable, and make sure he or she has the legal authority to do the eviction.

Some states require the owner to pay to have the tenant's belongings in storage for a period of time. If your state has this requirement, find a constable with a warehouse to serve the eviction notice, conduct the move-out, and store the belongings.

In those states where a tenant's belongings can be stored on the sidewalk, make sure the constable does this carefully. You want the tenant's belongings to be placed on the sidewalk in a formal manner, not strewn around as if the tenant has no right to dignity.

In any case, make sure the constable carries the appropriate liability insurance to protect against being sued by the tenant. You also prefer the tenant to sue the constable or sheriff, not your insurance policy, if something goes wrong with an eviction.

BE PREPARED FOR A RESTRAINING ORDER

After going to court and losing, the tenant, in some states, might have the option of appealing the judge's decision. It could be taken to a higher court. You would then have to defend your case all over again in a higher court, in front of a different judge.

There are several reasons why you might have to go back to court. The tenant might miss going to court because of some emergency. Having missed his or her day in court, the tenant has the right to reschedule the court appearance.

You might have to go to court during the eviction itself. The tenant in some states has the right to ask for a temporary restraining order to prevent you from completing the eviction until he or she is heard in court again. She can file for a new amount of time to find another apartment. How much extra time she will get will depend on your argument and the tenant's needs. If she has small children, she might get as much as another ten days to move on her own. You can petition for the writ of possession again.

One reason for a restraining order might be that the tenant has gotten all the rent money together. He or she will go to court with the money in hand and ask the judge to reconsider the eviction based on the new "evidence." In this case, the court will call you, the homeowner, and have you stop the eviction, go to court, and accept the rent money.

If nonpayment of rent were the reason you received the eviction notice and the tenant has all the money plus court costs, you would have little reason, if any, to refuse the money and continue the eviction. There might have to be some discussion about the constable and moving costs incurred. This would be a good reason to have an attorney working for you. Still, the court clerks will walk you through the process.

STAY AWAY FROM THE TENANT

Sometimes, before the eviction day, the tenant will try to make a last-ditch effort to convince you to stop the move-out. Whether it comes in the form of a threat, crying, begging, or even money, it will be an emotional trap for you. For nonpayment of rent, unless the tenant has all the money, including court costs, in the form of a certified check or cash (the tenant can put a stop-payment on a money order), you should not stop the eviction.

Do not interact with the tenant. If you have an attorney, give his or her telephone number to the tenant. Do this even if the tenant is paying every dime of the rent and court costs. Your attorney needs to know how to protect your rights in this situation. Let the tenant call your attorney and discuss the rent money with him or her.

If for other than nonpayment of rent, let your tenant know that any communication about the eviction and what happens are to be held with your lawyer. If you do not have an attorney, tell the tenant that you can discuss the eviction in court. Any agreement, discussion, or the like should have taken place or been resolved before you started the legal action.

HAVE THE KEYS OR A LOCKSMITH READY

Have the keys to the apartment available for the constable or sheriff to use. If you are not going to attend the eviction, make sure the keys work.

At some point before the eviction day, you should find out whether the tenant has changed the apartment locks and no key is available. Do a visual check of the apartment lock to see if it is the same cylinder you installed on the door. Is there now a second lock on the door, one you did not provide to the tenant? If it appears that you may not have a key to the unit, call a locksmith and inform the constable or sheriff of the possible situation in advance of the eviction.

If the tenant has placed a lock that is secured and cannot be duplicated or picked open, allow the constable to break into the apartment to gain access. Make sure it is opened through the lock, not by punching a hole in the door.

Sometimes, the constable will ask whether the tenant has already moved out. This often happens before the eviction is supposed to take place, when the tenant wants to prevent the eviction from becoming a public record by moving out on his or her own.

BE PREPARED FOR A DIFFICULT EVICTION

You never know how an eviction will end. Anything and everything can happen. During my years as a property manager, I was exposed to and attended evictions that have made me angry, frustrated, frightened, and even made my heart hurt. I have evicted tenants that could not leave fast enough for me or anyone else associated with the case. But, I never did an eviction that made me happy.

Prepare for the tenant to be frustrated and angry. I used to go to my evictions but stopped when I realized my presence added fuel to the fire. The landlord or property manager is the last person the tenant wants to see as his or her belongings are being packed up and hauled on a truck or left on the sidewalk.

If the tenant was someone I liked or was elderly or infirm, I felt bad. That is not good for business, which is why you should let the constable and his professional movers do the work.

Case #1

As the site manager, I went with the constable with the keys to the apartment. After knocking on the door for quite some time, the tenant greeted us from the inside the apartment door. He said he had a gun and dared the constable to open the door. His family and the police were called. The standoff lasted hours as we tried to convince the tenant to come out and let the process happen.

After the police, newscasters, and television cameras left, we found out that the eviction was the end of a long line of bad luck for the tenant. It was losing his home that sent him over the edge.

This is why you must use a constable or sheriff to complete a move-out eviction. You never know what awaits you behind the door of a tenant about to be evicted. Give him or her the keys and leave.

Case #2

One tenant came to my office and cried profusely, asking me to allow him his dignity by not using a constable with a large truck to move him out. His neighbors were outside, watching it all happen. He was extremely embarrassed. Because the eviction was already in progress, there was nothing I could (or would) do to stop the proceedings.

I made a mental note that all this could have been avoided if the tenant had worked with me during the eviction process, instead of taking a cavalier and dismissive attitude during each phase of the case. An eviction is a serious matter. The situation became a reality to him only when he saw his personal belongings packed up and taken away by a bunch of strangers. I reminded myself that I was not doing the eviction — he had evicted himself.

Case #3

One of the most heart-wrenching evictions I ever attended was that of a nice, churchgoing woman and her two young children. The apartment building, owned by a church, had strong metal apartment doors more than 3 inches thick. When we arrived at the apartment, we discovered that the tenant had changed the locks to the door before we arrived. She must have jammed something in the lock, because the locksmith could not open it.

We were forced to use a large sledgehammer to break the cylinder lock on the door. It was similar to what the police use when they do drug raids. This took about half an hour. The entire time, we could hear the tenant and the children singing church hymns inside the apartment.

When we finally got the door open, we saw the tenant and her two children sitting directly in front of the apartment door, waiting for us to come in. They never moved from their seats the entire time the men were packing up their belongings. They had a quiet dignity that moved me, even though this had been a difficult case to win. I left and called the church to have someone go to the unit and assist the tenant and her family. I never attended another eviction from that day on.

REMOVE AND STORE YOUR EVICTED TENANT'S BELONGINGS

You have won your case in court and have the eviction notice in your hand. Finally, you think, you have finished spending time, money, and emotions on the eviction process. At this point, you may not care what happens to the tenant's belongings. You just want them out of your place. Unfortunately, this is the beginning of the next phase of your eviction — removing the tenant's belongings from your property.

Before you start the eviction process, you should research and plan the process from beginning to end. Each phase of a residential eviction carries with it an action, a time period, and obligations of law and money. If you have won your case, the court will mail the eviction of judgment to you. By that time, you should already know the laws in your state regarding the removal and storage of an evicted tenant's belongings. This is your responsibility and obligation as the property owner.

There are guidelines and actions a property owner should take as due diligence for his or her property. These guidelines do not overrule taking the required legal action regarding the removal of tenant belongings. Most states, such as Massachusetts, do not allow you to rent a U-Haul truck and remove your tenant's belongings on your own. This is the job of the constable or sheriff you must hire and pay to do the moving of furniture. Do not even change the locks to the apartment until the constable has completed the eviction and posted the legal notice on the apartment door.

There are states that require you to remove and store your tenant's belongings at your expense. Each state dictates how long the homeowner must pay for warehousing. The rate for storage of an evicted tenant's belongings should not be more than what the warehouse normally charges.

The tenant is notified in advance by the constable of the date and time the physical eviction will take place. Coordinate this information between you and the constable so that the constable is given the keys to the unit for that day and time. Do not be in a hurry to "convince" the tenant to leave on his or her own by cutting off the utilities. This is illegal almost everywhere. Take the time to do it right the first time.

If you have reason to believe the tenant has moved out permanently on his or her own, you need to write a letter to that effect to the tenant's last known address, with a copy under the unit door. Give a 48-hour notice for the tenant to let you know whether he or she still lives in the apartment, or you will enter and reclaim the unit by changing the locks. Be reasonable — if it appears that some items have been left for a last pickup (bed or cabinets, for example), give it another day. It will be cheaper than fighting in small-claims court about the value of what you threw out. Take pictures before you throw items away, preferably before you bag it up.

The following suggestions, I believe, just make good business practice. All it takes is one calamity with a tenant, and your eviction could start all over.

1. Take care in hiring your constable or sheriff. You may use his or her services more than once in the lifetime of owning your property. Have a discussion about how he or she performs the duties. What does he or she do if the tenant becomes hostile? Does he or she perform talk-out evictions? A talk-out eviction is one in which the constable convinces the tenant to move out before he or she has to execute the writ of possession. It is cheaper than an actual move-out, and the tenant does not have an eviction on his or her public record.

2. Make sure your constable or sheriff is fully bonded and insured. Get it in writing in the form of a certificate of insurance. If the constable uses staff to move out the tenant belongings, he or she should have worker's compensation insurance. If a warehouse is used, the constable should have liability insurance, fire, and theft. If something bad happens to the tenant's belongings during the move-out or after being warehoused, you want the constable's insurance company to be sued, not your homeowner's insurance. If the sheriff or constable carries a gun, ask for a copy of its registration as a legal firearm.

3. Have a written contract with your constable that absolves you from liability once the constable or sheriff enters your house. The physical eviction move-out is his responsibility. Give him the key to the building and apartment, or let him into the unit yourself, and let him do his job.

4. Have a plan for what will be done with items the constable will not take, such as food, plants, pets, or illegal drugs. Review your emergency contact information form for the name, address, and telephone number of the tenant's next of kin in case the totally unforeseen occurs, such as a child under the age of 18 years being left in the apartment on the day of the eviction.

There are states where the owner must store the tenant's belongings in a bonded warehouse, as opposed to putting them on the sidewalk. Here are some reasonable guidelines for you and your constable:

- The tenant should be informed in writing where the belongings have been taken and stored. A copy of the eviction notice should be attached to the apartment door for the tenant to know why the locks have been changed. The business name, address, and business telephone of the constable or sheriff should be provided.

- All the property is to be removed at the same time. All property is to go to the warehouse, unless the tenant wants the property to go somewhere else.

- The tenant has the right to be able to get to where the belongings are stored. The constable should be instructed to store the tenant's belongings within a reasonable distance of the former housing.

- The warehouse must be public, fully bonded, licensed, and insured.

- The tenant should be given the business name, address, and telephone number of the warehouse where the belongings have been stored.

- The tenant should be informed in writing how long the belongings will be stored at the warehouse and that they can be sold at auction after that date. The warehouse may keep any proceeds of the auction to cover any unpaid storage fees.

- The notice should include advisement that it is the tenant's obligation to tell the warehouse of his or her new address.

- In most states that require warehousing, the constable must file a list of what was removed from the apartment to the housing court after the eviction. You and the tenant should also get a copy.

You might think all this is unnecessary, but you could pay for noncompliance in your state with a triple-damage lawsuit. Again, it is your responsibility as the property owner to know the state laws regarding the proper way to remove, store, and/or dispose of your evicted tenant's belongings. This information is available through your attorney. It can also be found at your local library; statehouse bookstore; online under a search such as "[name of state] eviction storage laws;" at a legal Web site, such as **www. nolo.com**; or at a landlord information Web site, such as **www. mrlandlord.com**.

MAKE SURE EVERYTHING GOES

Tenants will sometimes leave things in the apartment that they do not want anymore or do not have time to remove. You do not want them either, so preparations have to be made to ensure that everything goes during the eviction. The constable should be told to take everything in the apartment, whether the tenant wants the item or not. Your vacant apartment is not a storage facility, nor is this an opportunity for the tenant to do his or her spring cleaning on your dime.

Make sure the tenant takes pets, food, and flowers. These are perishable goods that the constable cannot store in the warehouse. I once had a tenant move out and leave a large cage with eight live hamsters in the vacant apartment. When my maintenance supervisor brought it to me, there was no food or water in the cage. Furthermore, the cage had not been changed in a while.

After we fed and watered them and changed the bottom of the cage, we quickly looked for a kind soul to take them off our hands. We were lucky. After the word got out, a teacher took them for her elementary school classroom. You do not want to inherit a tenant's animals after you have removed the tenant.

You are paying for a tenant to be totally evicted from the apartment straight to the warehouse. Side trips are the responsibility of the tenant. If the constable is willing to do this, make sure he knows that it is the tenant who will pay for the side trip(s).

Below are some actions to take if you are left with perishable items in the apartment after the eviction and the tenant has not shown up:

Food: Throw it all away. It is worth any extra cost to have the constable do this during the course of the eviction.

Plants: Keep them in your office or home, give them away, or throw them away.

Pets: Review your resident emergency information form (see Appendix) for the next of kin. Contact and get them to pick up the pet(s). Otherwise, take it to the local animal shelter.

Exotic animals: Again, refer to the resident emergency information form and call the contacts to take the animals. Or, take these animals to the local animal shelter, or call the zoo to see if it would like an additional snake for its collection.

The constable or sheriff must leave a copy of the official notice that the eviction has been completed posted on the front apartment door so that it does not fall off. The eviction is not considered complete until the constable returns the eviction notice to the court. Once it is returned as an executed eviction, it will be posted on the court record books and made available to the public. This is where other credit bureaus for landlords will pick up the information for their clients across the nation.

SECURE THE UNIT

Chances are, you will not get the key back from your evicted tenant. Change the locks to the apartment door as soon as possible so no one can get back in after the eviction. This should be done during the eviction move, while the constable is moving out the tenant's belongings. You do not want anyone with a key to come back later to vandalize the apartment out of anger.

21 TIE UP LOOSE ENDS

Y ou are not finished after you have evicted your tenant. When your tenant and his or her belongings are all out of your apartment, you can put a period on your landlord/tenant relationship. Still, there will be some loose ends to resolve.

REVIEW WHAT YOU ARE ENTITLED TO RECOVER

If you get a court eviction, you can recover only what is on that eviction execution document. If you give a 30-day notice to quit and the tenant moves out on his or her own after receiving your eviction notice in the middle of the month, the tenant still owes rent for the remainder of the month.

If the tenant left the apartment in bad shape, your costs could far exceed the rent for the month. You may be able to recover some of your costs of the vacant apartment from your homeowner's insurance policy. Call your agent and explain your situation.

FINAL APARTMENT INSPECTION

After the eviction has been completed and the locks changed, go through the apartment and complete a written or videotape inspection. This should be done the same day as the eviction or the day you know the tenant has moved out.

If a constable or sheriff completed the eviction, chances are that everything was taken out and no damage to the apartment was done.

There are times when the tenant will move out on his or her own. This is done to avoid having the eviction a matter of record in the court system. The tenant, angry at being evicted, will sometimes do damage to the apartment to "get back" at the owner or management company. Here is one example of an act of retaliation faced after an eviction move:

The evicted tenant had several dogs, which was the reason for the eviction. She moved out on her own, but before leaving the apartment, she smeared dog defecation all over the walls. The floors were loaded with urine and feces, apparently in the dogs' bedroom. In addition, the tenant wrote an obscene message in defecation on one wall for the manager who evicted her. It took a good deal of money, ammonia, and face masks to get the apartment back in renting shape.

An angry or vengeful tenant will sometimes break up and destroy everything that cannot move and leave it in the apartment before being evicted, including your appliances, kitchen cabinets, and anything else in an effort to "get back" at you.

Some tenants will have a big party the night before their eviction. When the truck arrives, we have sometimes found partygoers still in the apartment with the tenant, sleeping in beds or on couches and certainly not ready to be evicted. Upon inspection, it was apparent that table manners and bathroom etiquette had not been a major concern of anyone at the party. We proceeded with the eviction, removing not only her belongings, but also the tenant and her guests from the apartment.

VACANCY MAINTENANCE

Expect to get the apartment back on a paying basis in the next 30 days. Use any reserve funds you have to get the apartment rented. If you cannot do that, then you need to see if your homeowner's insurance policy can help with some of the costs. Lost rent can never be recovered.

- Do not leave the apartment dirty and unkempt after the eviction. Clean it up and throw away the debris to keep insects and vermin from taking over.

- Put the utilities in your name until you have another tenant. This is a tax-deductible expense. Keep the utilities on so your contractors have light, heat or air conditioning, and water to work.

- Do pest control on the apartment while you are fixing it up. If there is a problem, you can eliminate it and clean up the carcasses before showing the apartment.

- How long do you intend to keep the apartment empty? If the apartment will be vacant during the winter, you will need to protect it from the elements. If you can, you want to get the apartment back on line the same month of the eviction. You want to rent it out the first of the next month.

- Keep every receipt of work done on the vacant apartment

in one place or file folder marked for that apartment, including canceled checks. You will need them to justify your expenses taken from the tenant's security deposit. You will also need those same receipts for your income taxes as apartment maintenance expenses.

• When you write checks to pay for repairs to the vacant apartment, even to contractors and vendors, write "vacant apt #2 repairs" on the note section of the check. You will be able to separate those checks with ease every month or at tax time.

SECURITY DEPOSIT REFUND REPORT

When the tenant is no longer in your apartment, you must file and supply the tenant with a security deposit refund letter. This letter notifies the tenant whether he or she will get money returned from the security deposit, how much, and if not returned, why. You should have maintained the security deposit in an interest-bearing bank account for this occasion.

Do the refund paperwork in the required number of days after the eviction or move-out. Consult your attorney, or get a copy of the security deposit law in your state from the statehouse bookstore. Notification requirements could be as few as five days after a tenant has moved out, or as many as 30 days. This is important to do on time, because in some states, failure to send the tenant a security deposit accounting in the required time for your state could result in a fine of more than three times the amount of the security deposit, payable to the tenant.

If you keep the entire security deposit, or even a portion, you must give an accounting of every expense you made in the apartment, minus wear and tear items. This accounting must be included with the security deposit letter. The move-out apartment inspection form should be attached to the security deposit letter.

Expect the evicted tenant to protest. To counter this, keep all receipts from vendors who did any work in the apartment; keep all canceled checks of work performed and paid for; especially keep receipts of cash payments made for soap, window cleanser, and toilet cleanser, if you do the work yourself. Again, you cannot deduct wear and tear repairs from the security deposit.

Better yet, take a picture of the entire apartment before you complete paint and repairs and again after the work is done. Then, if the evicted tenant files a small-claims case against you, you have all the written and picture evidence to present before the judge to defend why you kept the security deposit.

Finally, in some states, you must still pay any interest due the tenant from the security deposit. Include that money in the final security deposit refund report. You can subtract any damages from the interest amount.

If you have kept the money in an interest-bearing savings account, you should close out that account, subtract what you are due, and send a check for the remainder to the tenant's last known address or send an invoice with a copy of all your supporting documents with it. Keep the originals with you in the tenant file folder.

Call your constable to see if he or she has a new address for the tenant. You can also do a new credit report to get an updated address to send the security deposit refund letter. You are allowed to do this because when you had the tenant complete a rental application, you notified the tenant on the form and had the tenant initial that you are allowed to check his or her credit report for purposes of verifying information before and after the tenancy but only for information relating to the tenancy.

Go Back to Court

Make sure you note when your permission to evict your tenant will be issued. Some judges will not provide you with this document for up to three months, depending upon the circumstances of the case. For example, if there are really severe or prolonged weather conditions, like a series of snowstorms, and the tenant truly has nowhere else to live, the judge may hold the execution until the tenant can be placed in a shelter. No one wants to see a tenant with children removed from a property and their belongings set on the sidewalk, under twenty-degree weather conditions. If you have a lawyer, he or she will track down your execution (formal court permission to evict). If you did the eviction yourself, you may have to go back to housing court to find out what happened to your execution.

If you received the apartment through your eviction notice, you can go back to court and file for damages done to your apartment by the tenant. Damages must be over the amount of the security deposit and must be itemized in detail for the judge.

File your small-claims case as soon as the eviction has taken place. You will need to serve the ex-tenant where he or she currently lives. Have the constable who performed the eviction give you the forwarding address. If you file your case in the first 30 days after the eviction, it will ensure the tenant has good service notification with a court date.

Due to stalking and battered women issues, the post office may not provide you with the forwarding address of your former tenant. Try anyway. Bring the tenant's lease and show your identification, indicating that you are only trying to give the ex-tenant proper notification regarding their security deposit status.

SMALL-CLAIMS COURT

During your annual apartment inspection, you might find that several parts of the apartment have been damaged. If a tenant has damaged your apartment, you do not necessarily have to evict the person or family. You can take the tenant to small-claims court. It is always better to take the tenant to small-claims court during the tenancy. This way, you will still have the security deposit available for when the tenant moves out. Also, you can use the failure to pay for damages as part of your eviction case or non-lease renewal.

The security deposit is supposed to be used for damages made during the life of the tenancy, but, the deposit might not be enough to cover the present damages. If you have had a long-term tenant for say, five years, you may have raised the rent but not the security deposit amount.

REPORT WHAT HAPPENED

If you want to see your former tenant again with money in his or her hands, report the eviction results to the three major credit bureaus. There is no guarantee that doing this will make the tenant pay you, but, it will alert other landlords that the tenant left your apartment owing rent money and/or damage reimbursements.

Some landlords do not know to use the credit bureau to report rent claims. Property managers will always report their evicted tenants. The three major credit bureaus (Equifax, Transunion, and Experian) are more than happy to take the information on the rent arrears case that you won and put the information in the tenant's file. Even if the tenant never pays your rent arrears, the amount will stay on his or her credit record for seven years. You can always reinstate your arrears to the credit bureaus after that time.

I have received money when the former tenant tried to buy a house, refinance a house already purchased, or get another apartment. You never know when a real estate or property management company will access a tenant's credit history. Get the information into the credit bureau system, and report what happened to you. You can file both unpaid rent and the cost of damages incurred in the unit. It should be the same amount as what you reported in the Security Deposit Refund Letter.

National Credit Bureaus

Experian Credit Union: **www.Experian.com**

Transunion Credit Union: **www.Transunion.com**

Equifax Credit Union: **www.Equifax.com**

LANDLORD REVENGE WITH REFERRALS

You have done your job, and the tenant has been moved out of the apartment. You have looked at the poor condition of the apartment, thought about all the money you spent on the apartment, going to court, and evicting the tenant. You have also added up how much it will cost to get the apartment back in shape. You are angry about the whole thing.

You might want to get even with the tenant, but revenge or retaliation is based on emotion and is a waste of time and effort. You have suffered a business loss, and you will do a better job the next time you rent the apartment. What is important is to get the unit back on a paying track.

You might breathe a sigh of relief that you will not have to deal with this tenant ever again, but the tenant still needs another apartment. Expect some of your evicted tenants to use you as a referral.

This might not be a bad idea. If you had to evict your tenant through no fault of his or her own, such as the inability to pay your recent rent increase, you will not want to jeopardize the tenant's ability to find a cheaper place to live.

Watch out though, if you are still angry when another landlord calls for a referral for a tenant you had to fight to get rid of. You might want to be vindictive and tell everything, but this could get you sued for slander if the landlord or manager tells the former tenant what you said. You want to be honest and fair; just give the facts.

The most frequent question you will be asked is, "Would you rent to this tenant again?" If the answer is no, say so. If the reason has nothing to do with you or the tenant but was due to the tenant's circumstances, I think you should say so. The tenant might be applying for an apartment that is less expensive than your rent.

You Might See Your Tenant Again

As I have stated throughout this book, an eviction is an adversarial situation. That does not necessarily mean you have to have an adversarial relationship with your tenant. You should be able to evict a tenant and still be able to relate to him or her afterward. If you allow the tenant to leave with dignity and have treated the person with respect during his or her stay, you will be able to move out a tenant or family and still be able to sleep well at night.

I have run into former tenants of mine months and even years after I had evicted them. Some have even been grateful that I evicted them. For some of my tenants, the eviction was a wake-up call that their life had gone terribly wrong. Others who left the apartment were able to get their lives together, find a better job, and eventually, a better apartment. Several bought houses to avoid ever having to experience the eviction process again.

Of course, there will be those tenants whom you will not want to ever see again, and that feeling will be mutual from the tenant's point of view. It is a small world, where there is never a guarantee that paths will not cross again. This is yet another reason why you should always keep your cool and try to get through the eviction process with as little trauma and drama as possible.

Sometimes They Come Back

Let us suppose you have successfully evicted a bad tenant. It took you months to start the eviction, go to court, and win your case. You lost money by not getting the monthly rent before and during the eviction. You spent money hiring a constable and paying court fees. You will lose money from the vacant apartment you have to fix up. Now you discover the evicted tenant is regularly visiting the property.

Why would an evicted tenant want to return to the place where he or she was thrown out? It is possible the tenant is living with another tenant in the building. Is the evicted tenant related to a current tenant? Was it a drug eviction? If so, there are situations where the drug dealer will continue to visit the property until he can contact his "customers" and advise them of his new location.

Sometimes the evicted tenant will return because he or she has nowhere else to go. If the tenant did not have the rent money for you, chances are the tenant does not have the money to rent another apartment.

There are cases where the tenant, still holding the keys to the entry door, will break into the apartment. This is why you should always work diligently to make the necessary painting and repairs to rent the apartment as soon as possible. You should also visit your vacancy often, at least once a week. Those on your street who know you have a vacant apartment could decide to break in and remove valuables, such as the kitchen cabinets, copper pipes, or the toilet.

You need to let the former tenant know that he or she is no longer wanted at your property. You should let your current tenants know this too, if they have not already gotten the news. Sometimes an owner, visiting the property, will see the former tenant going in or coming out of the building. Inform the person that if he or she continues to visit your property, you will get a restraining order legally forbidding the tenant from entering your building. Tell the tenant that if he or she is found at the building again, you will call the police.

To get a forwarding address to send the restraining order to, contact your constable or sheriff who did the eviction. He or she will need the forwarding address of your tenant because of the stored items in the warehouse. If furniture was put on the sidewalk, sometimes the constable will get tenant information from a friend in the building. You can also run another credit check on the tenant to see whether there is an updated address.

Make a formal complaint at the local police station, contact the local drug enforcement unit, and ask for temporary additional patrols. Evicted tenants might also try to rent your vacant apartment through another tenant, friend, or relative. Screen your next rental applicants carefully.

A SELF-INVENTORY

It is not always easy to own and maintain rental income property. Doing paperwork, preventing potential liabilities, making repairs, collecting rent, and monitoring behaviors in your house or investment property is an ongoing business. The eviction process is an extended, financial, and draining part of the business of home ownership.

An eviction is a serious matter, and it should be the remedy of last resort. Emphasis should be placed on preventing an eviction, if possible. You cannot make a profit from your real estate investment if you are spending it putting people in and out of your building(s).

What went wrong? If you had it to do over again, what would you do differently? These questions must be contemplated at length and answered before you rent the apartment again.

Regardless of your answers, one change should be resolute. Before you rent to another tenant, keep a separate, interest-bearing savings account funded with profits from your rents for emergencies and evictions. Do not be left at the mercy of a bad tenant because you cannot afford to cover the rent or hire a lawyer.

Below is a summary of some of the property management tips in this book:

- Spend more time, attention, and money making sure you have chosen a good tenant before the tenant moves into your apartment.

- Have policies regarding payment of rent and tenant behavior included in your lease.

- Maintain a file folder on each tenant, with all the tenant's paperwork in it.

- Never make verbal agreements with your tenant.

- Follow your policies to the letter.

- Know your lease and make your tenant read the lease.

- Inspect each of your tenant's apartments at least once a year, and write down its condition for your files.

- Keep all receipts of canceled checks, vendor work, and supplies purchased to make repairs at the property in one file.

- Act sooner rather than later regarding the eviction process; situations rarely get better if you do not take any action.

- Stay away from revenge or retaliation thoughts. Keep a calm head during the eviction process.

- Document everything that might support your eviction claim.

- Practice "Preventive Anticipation" by writing and filing an incident report about issues and problems that go on at the property that might come back later as a lawsuit or defense to your lawsuit(s).

- Prepare for the eviction in advance.

- Keep a timely follow-up of eviction deadline dates.

- Do not allow your tenant to intimidate you with threats or insinuations. You control your apartments and your building, not the tenant.

- Do not take any retaliatory action against the tenant for any reason.

- Keep your paperwork and documentation organized.

- Do not take the law into your own hands.

- Let your lawyer do your talking for you.

- Report to the credit bureaus any tenants who leave owing rent and/or damage monies.

- Never stop an eviction until you accomplish your goal(s).

- File the ex-tenant's security deposit report in the next two weeks, have it sent to the last known address, and keep a copy.

- Report the ex-tenant to the three major credit bureaus.

- Stay professional throughout the entire process. This is business, never personal, even if the tenant is a friend or relative.

There is plenty of good information about the eviction process available at every library and at your city and state courthouses. Every homeowner or investor with tenants should have a copy of the state security deposit law, condominium law, state sanitary or building code law, and this book as landlord/tenant referral tools.

Call your city hall and statehouse bookstore to have free housing information mailed to you. The Internet is also a valuable and time-saving way to get information on laws in your state.

BIOGRAPHY

Carolyn Gibson is a Certified Property Manager® (CPM®) who writes about what she has learned from her decades of accomplishments and professional experiences in the residential property management business. Her first book was the successful *How to Pick The Best Tenant* (1st Books Library). It is a guide to the best ways to screen and select a new tenant.

Carolyn established her eviction credentials by evicting tenants in her early years as a property manager, without the benefit of an attorney. She worked her way up in the property management industry, starting as a maintenance supervisor and eventually becoming a director of management. She established her own property management company in Boston, Massachusetts, where she managed market-rate residential properties, government-subsidized properties, condominiums, rooming houses, and low income tax credit and public housing. Carolyn is now working in consulting, seminar workshops, and training and speaking engagements.

Carolyn is a member of and former instructor with the internationally recognized trade organization the Institute of Real Estate Management (IREM®). She has given IREM many years of service as a member, local and national committee chairperson, and co-chair of the organization. She is a former president of the Boston IREM Chapter #4 and a former regional vice-president for New England.

She has been featured in the *New England Real Estate Journal,* the national trade publication *Journal of Property Management,* the *Boston Globe, Boston Herald,* and on Boston cable television and radio talk shows. Her Web site contributions can be found at her Web site and at **www.ezinearticles.com**, **www.WomensRadio.com**, **www.searchwarp.com**, **www.articlesbase.com**, **www.lifetips.com**, and **www.helium.com**.

Ms. Gibson, a native and resident of Boston, Massachusetts, is a Simmons College graduate. Visit her Web site at **www.Synergy-professionals.com**.

APPENDIX

FORMS

MONIES RECEIVED FOR USE AND OCCUPANCY LETTER

Date: _____

Address: _____

_____

Apt. #: _____

Dear _____:

We have received your recent payment of $_____ by money order/
check # _____ on _____ 20_____.

Please be advised that:

1. This payment and all future payments will be applied either on arrears balances and/or for use and occupancy. This payment and all future payments are not accepted as rent.

2. The owner of the property is not relinquishing or waiving its right under the notice of termination served upon you or under the lease. Rather, all of its rights in connection with said notice and said lease are hereby reserved.

3. Your landlord does not intend to create a new tenancy by acceptance of this amount or by the acceptance of all future payments since they are not accepted as rent but on the account of the payment of arrearage and/or for use of occupancy only.

4. This may be the last notice that you will receive concerning future payments. All future payments will be accepted as outlined above regardless of any notation on your check or money order and regardless of any further delivery of letters similar to this one.

_____   cc: Tenant file

Title: _____   Section 8 leasing officer (if applicable)

RENT PAYMENT AGREEMENT

Date: _____

Address: _____ Apt. #: _____

_____

Agreement to Pay Rent Arrears

I, _____, living on _____
Apt. # _____ in _____, (state) _____,
acknowledge that my rent is in arrears this date a total of $_____.

I agree to pay $_____ (per month) or $_____ (per week)
on my arrears until my rent arrears is paid in full.

I also agree to continue to pay my regular monthly rent of $_____ by
the 5th business day of each month. If I am a Section 8 certificate or voucher
subsidy holder, I realize that the amount of my regular rent could change as part
of the recertification process during the period while I am paying both current
and arrears rent.

I understand that the owner or management still reserves the legal right to
continue the eviction action at its discretion. *All monies received will be for use
and occupancy only as long as I have a rent balance.* The owner/management
agent reserves its legal rights throughout this agreement, if not broken by the
resident _____ (initial).

_____   _____
Resident name   Co-resident name
Date: _____   Date: _____

_____   _____
Management agent rep.   Property owner name
Date: _____   Date: _____

Please complete both copies and return one copy to the owner/manager.

cc: Resident file
     Section 8 leasing officer
     Attorney

264

TENANT/PROPERTY INCIDENT REPORT

Date of the incident: _____ 20_____

Time of the incident: _____ a.m./p.m.

Location of the incident: _____

Apt. #: _____

Who was involved? _____

_____

_____

What happened? _____

_____

_____

_____

Any witnesses? If yes, who? _____

_____

Where do they live? _____

_____

Insurance adjuster contacted? _____

Fire department contacted? _____

Police department contacted? _____

Action or follow-up? _____

_____

_____

Who prepared this report? _____

cc: Tenant file
    Attorney
    Insurance company
    Section 8 leasing officer (if applicable)

RESIDENT WORK ORDER REQUEST FORM

Work order #: _____ Date: _____ 20 _____

Telephone: (_____) _____ E-mail: _____

Resident: _____

Address: _____

Apt. #: _____ City: _____ State: _____ Zip:_____

Resident gives permission to enter? _____ Yes _____ No

Repairs needed: _____
_____
_____
_____

Repairs completed:_____
_____
_____
_____

Resident signature of satisfaction: _____

******************** **For Landlord Use Only** ********************

Is a specialist needed? _____ What kind? _____

Name of the person who completed the repair: _____
_____

Time to complete repair: _____ Date completed: _____ 20___

Was it resident damage? _____ Cost of materials: $_____

Supplies purchased from: _____

Purchase order number used: _____

Homeowner name/company: _____

Address:_____
_____

City: _____ State: _____ Zip: _____

Phone: (_____) _____ - _____

RESIDENT DAMAGE LETTER

Dear Resident:

This is a bill for work and/or repairs dated _____, 20_____ for:

_____ Lost apartment keys/lockout during work hours
Labor/materials

_____ Lost apartment keys/ lockout after work hours
Labor/materials

_____ Changed apartment lock(s) at request of the resident
Labor/materials

_____ Broken, torn, or missing window screen
Labor/materials

_____ Found and removed an object from the toilet and/or sink
Cost: $_____

_____ Replaced shade(s) in one year of occupancy
Cost: $ _____ each

_____ Broken hollow-core door in unit (labor and materials)
Cost: $ _____ each

_____ Replaced a light globe inside the unit
Cost: $ _____

Other damage: _____
_____

We are billing you because the repairs __needed/made__ are considered more than what we consider as normal wear and tear work.

You owe $_____ for materials & $_____ for labor, totaling $_____.

Please make your payment by money order only to: _____
_____

If the amount is not paid by _____, 20_____, we have the right to pursue the amount owed through legal means. This date may provide you with a maximum of 30 days to pay, depending upon the amount owed.

If you have any questions concerning this bill, feel free to contact the owner or property manager at (_____) _____. E-mail: _____
_____

_____   cc: Resident file
Owner/Property manager   Section 8 leasing officer

BUILDING INSPECTION FORM

Condition as of: _____ , 20_____

Building address: _____
_____

Inspected by: _____

Work orders created: _____

OUTSIDE GROUNDS	GOOD	POOR	COMMENTS
Sidewalk			
Gutters			
Front yard			
Side/rear yard			
Parking lot			
Parking lot lines			
Driveway			
Fencing			
Dumpster/trash area			
Condition of Dumpsters			
Condition of trash cans			
Grass/shrubs/flowers			
Trees and branches			
Playground area			
Picnic area			
Interior			
Wheelchair lift tested			
First-floor hallway			
Second-floor hallway			
Third-floor hallway			
Fourth-floor hallway			
Ceiling globes			
Elevator walls			
Elevator tracks			
Fire doors			
Smoke detectors			

BUILDING INSPECTION FORM			
OUTSIDE GROUNDS	**GOOD**	**POOR**	**COMMENTS**
Fire doors			
Smoke detectors			
Fire extinguishers			
Railings and banisters			
Hallway radiators			
Roof door			
Exterior Areas			
Rear stains			
Front porch			
Back porch			
Brickwork			
Window sills			
Windows			
Front entry door			
Rear entry door			
Balconies			
Basement windows			
Doorbells			
Doorbell labels			
Mailboxes			
Mailbox labels			
Gutters/downspouts			
Floodlights			
Entry door lighting			
Number on the building			
Key keeper			
Graffiti on outside walls?			
Basement Area			
Lighting and ceiling			
Cleanliness			
Floors			
Windows			

BUILDING INSPECTION FORM			
OUTSIDE GROUNDS	GOOD	POOR	COMMENTS
Pipes covered with insulation?			
Any strong odors?			
Any leaks?			
Carbon monoxide detector			
Smoke detector			
Storage room			
Boiler room			
Hot water heaters			
Basement door secured			

APARTMENT INSPECTION FORM

Type of inspection: _____

Date of inspection: _____

Occupant's name: _____

Address: _____

Apt #: _____ # of Bedrooms: _____

	Tenant	Owner		
Refrigerator belongs to			Stove is gas ____ electric ____	
	Yes	No	Comments	
Insects/mice?				
Smoke detectors working				

Reception Area

	Pass	Fail	Damage	Comments
Condition of ceiling				
Condition of walls				
Condition of floor				
Condition of light fixtures				
Condition of wall outlets				
Condition of windows & screens				
Baseboard heat				

Master Bedroom

	Pass	Fail	Damage	Comments
Condition of ceiling				
Condition of walls				
Condition of floor				
Condition of light fixtures				
Condition of wall outlets				
Condition of windows & screens				
Baseboard heat				
Condition of doors				

APARTMENT INSPECTION FORM

Bedroom 2

	Pass	Fail	Damage	Comments
Condition of ceiling				
Condition of walls				
Condition of floor				
Condition of light fixtures				
Condition of wall outlets				
Condition of windows & screens				
Condition of shades				
Baseboard heat				
Condition of doors				

Bedroom 3

	Pass	Fail	Damage	Comments
Condition of ceiling				
Condition of walls				
Condition of floor				
Condition of light fixtures				
Condition of wall outlets				
Condition of windows & screens				
Condition of shades				
Baseboard heat				
Condition of doors				

Kitchen

	Pass	Fail	Damage	Comments
Condition of ceiling				
Condition of walls				
Condition of floor				
Condition of cabinets				
Condition of stove				
Condition of refrigerator				
Condition of light fixtures				

APARTMENT INSPECTION FORM

Kitchen Cont.

	Pass	Fail	Damage	Comments
Condition of wall fixtures				
Condition of pantry				
Condition of sink				
Condition of garbage disposal				

Living Room

Condition of ceiling				
Condition of walls				
Condition of floor				
Condition of light fixtures				
Condition of wall outlets				
Condition of windows & screens				
Heat thermostat				
Baseboard heat				
Condition of doors				

Bathroom

	Pass	Fail	Damage	Comments
Condition of ceiling				
Condition of walls				
Condition of floor				
Condition of tub/shower				
Condition of faucets				
Shower curtain rod				
Condition of windows				
Condition of toilet				
Condition of toilet seat				
Condition of sink				
Baseboard heat				

Comments: _____

_____

_____

APARTMENT INSPECTION FORM

Date of last painting: _____

General housekeeping comments: _____
_____
_____

Inspection by: _____
Title: _____

Tenant signature: _____
Date: _____

Work orders made up: _____
_____
_____
_____

SECURITY DEPOSIT REFUND REPORT

Date: _____, 20_____

Tenant Name: _____

Co-tenant: _____

Address: _____
Apt. #: _____ City _____ State: _____ Zip: _____

Date tenant moved in: _____, 20_____

Lease expiration date: _____, 20_____

Date tenant moved out: _____, 20_____

Date notice given: _____, 20_____

Reason for move out: _____

Repayment status:

Monthly rent: $_____

Unpaid rent due from _____ to _____
$_____

Remainder of lease rent due from _____ to _____
$_____

Security deposit/last month's rent

Amount of deposit: $_____

Interest due tenant from period _____ to _____
$_____

Unpaid rent: $_____

Keys not returned: $_____

Excessive cleaning: $_____ Explain: _____

Major repairs: $_____ Explain: _____

Eviction legal fees approved by court: $_____

Miscellaneous (explain) _____

Total security deposit deductions: $_____

Check due the owner by _____, 20_____:

$_____

RESIDENT EMERGENCY CONTACT INFORMATION FORM

We need to have a contact person for an emergency situation in your apartment. Please print your information.

Tenant name: _____

Address: _____

Apt #: _____ City: _____ State: _____ Zip: _____

Contacts:

Name: _____

Relationship: _____

Address: _____

City: _____ State: _____ Zip: _____

Work phone: (_____) _____

Home phone: (_____) _____

E-mail: _____

Name: _____

Relationship: _____

Address: _____

City: _____ State: _____ Zip: _____

Work phone: (_____) _____

Home phone: (_____) _____

E-mail: _____

Doctor's name: _____

Telephone: (_____) _____

Hospital/healthcare center: _____

City: _____

If you have a will or healthcare proxy, please give us information on the proxy, executrix, or administrator:

Name: _____

Relationship: _____

Address: _____

City: _____ State: _____ Zip: _____

Work phone: (_____) _____

Home phone: (_____) _____

E-mail: _____

Does anyone else have a key to your apartment for emergencies? _____

If yes, who? _____

Phone: (_____) _____

BIBLIOGRAPHY

1. National Association of Realtors (**www.realtor.org**)

2. *The MacArthur Foundation Newsletter*, Spring 2005 (**www.macfound.org**)

3. Tenant selection book, *How to Pick the Best Tenant*, by Carolyn Gibson (1st Books Library)

4. Number of days, weeks, and months change depending on your state eviction laws.

5. U.S. Census Bureau — 2006 American Community Survey (**www.factfinder.census.gov**)

6. Based on a 2007 $36,400 national average salary (**www.bls.gov**)

7. Some states, like Massachusetts, require the landlord to pay up to three months' storage of evicted tenant(s) belongings.

8. The Pioneer Institute (**www.Pioneerinstitute.org**) "Unemployment Insurance in Massachusetts"

9. Article source: **http://EzineArticles.com/?expert=Sheila_Webster-Heard**

10. Get a copy of your state's security deposit law for more information on pet deposits (**http://doglaw.hugpug.com**).

11. Legal Momentum — Housing Provisions 2006 (**www.legalmomentum.org**)

12. **www.hud.gov/offices/fheo/FHLaws/**

13. **www.defenselink.mil**

14. The New Jersey Assembly Housing and Local Government Committee, Senate Bill No. 1294

15. **www.hud.gov/offices/fheo/FHLaws/index.cfm**

References

How to Pick the Best Tenant
Author: Carolyn Gibson, CPM®
Paperback: 1st Edition, 212 pp
Publisher: 1st Books Library
December 2003
ISBN: 1-4107-66268
www.Synergyprofessionals.com

Government Assisted Housing: Professional Strategies for Site Managers
Author: Glenn L. French, CPM®
Paperback, 1st Edition, 250 pp
Publisher: Institute of Real Estate Management
December 1996
ISBN: 1-572030224
www.IREM.org

Stupid Mistakes of a Self-Made Millionaire Landlord
Author: Dan Arnold
Paperback, 1ˢᵗ Edition, 199 pp
Publisher: **www.danlingroup.com**
2007
Order directly from the author

Pacific Heights — (1990) DVD version available.

"Housing Rights for Survivors of Domestic Violence Living in Public Housing or Using Vouchers"
Legal Momentum
2006
www.legalmomentum.org

"Evicting Your Tenant Special Report"
June 2007
www.landlord.com

Every Dog's Legal Guide: A Must-Have Book for Your Owner
Author: Mary Randolph, J.D.
Paperback, 6th Edition, 352 pp
Publisher: **www.nolo.com**
October 2007
ISBN # 9781413307030

Everybody's Guide to Small Claims Court
Author: Ralph Warner, Esq.
Paperback, 11th Edition, 464 pp
Publisher: **www.nolo.com**
June 2006
ISBN # 9781413304909

Represent Yourself in Court: How to Prepare & Try a Winning Case
Author: Paul Bergman, Esq. & Sara J. Berman-Barrett, Esq.
Paperback, 5th Edition, 544 pp
Publisher: **www.nolo.com**
November 2005
ISBN # 9781413303698

Landlording on Auto-Pilot: A Simple, No-Brainer System for Higher Profits and Fewer Headaches
Author: Mike Butler
Paperback, 1st Edition, 242 pp
Publisher: Wiley
August 2006
ISBN # 04-7178-978X
www.mikebutler.com

The California Landlord's Law Book: Evictions
Author: David Wayne Brown
Paperback, 12th Edition, 363 pp plus CD-ROM
Publisher: Nolo
January 2007
ISBN-10 # 1-4133-05708
www.nolo.com

Evictions From The Inside
Author: Terry L. Searcy
Paperback, 1st Edition, 106 pp
Publisher: Terry & Terri Books
January 2000
ISBN-10 # 0-9676-91702

The Turnkey Investor's Rental Property Repossession (The Audio Program): How to Remove Deadbeat Tenants From Your Property Without Lawyers or Going to Eviction Court!
Author: Matthew S. Chan
Audio CD, 1st Edition
Publisher: Ascend Beyond Publishing
October 2006
ISBN-10 # 1-9337-2305

The Landlord's Trouble Shooter: A Survival Guide for New Landlords
Author: Robert Irwin
Paperback, 3rd Edition, 304 pp
Publisher: Kaplan Business
September 2004
ISBN-10 # 0-7931-86013
www.robertirwin.com

The Landlord's Financial Tool Kit
Author: Michael C. Thomsett
Paperback, 1st Edition, 256 pp
Publisher: American Management Association
September 2004
ISBN # 08-1447-2354
http://thomsettpublishing.blogspot.com

The Successful Landlord
Author: Ken Roth
Paperback, 1st Edition, 288 pp
Publisher: American Management Association
March 2004
ISBN # 08-1447-2281

The Property Management Toolkit
Author: Mike Beirne
Paperback, 1st Edition, 320 pp
Publisher: American Management Association
August 2006
ISBN # 08-1447-3512
www.mikebeirne.net

Information on Property Management

- **www.synergyprofessionals.com**

- **www.therealestatelibrary.com**

- **www.mrlandlord.com**

- **www.landlord.com**

- **www.thecreativeinvestor.com**

- **www.stupidmistakesbook.com**

- **www.apartments.com**

Government Based Web Sites

- **www.ada.gov** — Americans with Disabilities Act home page. Order a free copy of the Act on CD.

- **www.hud.gov** — U.S. Department of Housing & Urban Development (HUD) (Section 8 policies, voucher, and fair housing information)

Property Management Computer Software

- **www.tenantpro.com**

- **www.quickbookspro.com**

- **www.rentmanager.com**

- **www.tenantfile.com**

- **www.rent-right.com**

Legal Information

- **www.nolo.com** — National information on legal, business, real estate, family law, and human resources

- **www.legalmomentum.org** — Information on domestic violence and eviction of tenants using a Section 8 Voucher

- **www.advantagetenant.com** — Provides information on landlord and tenant law in all 50 states

- **www.legalzoom.com** — Legal forms information

- **www.freeadvice.com** — Legal landlord/tenant law by state

- **www.rentlaw.com** — A national landlord/tenant legal Web site

- **www.thelpa.com** — A national landlord/tenant legal Web site

Property Management Trade Organizations

- **www.irem.org** — Institute of Real Estate Management, National Office

- **www.naahq.org** — National Apartment Association

- **www.caionline.org** — Community Associations Institute

- **www.boma.org** — Builders, Owners & Managers Association

- **www.nchm.org** — National Center for Housing Management

- **www.landlording101.com** — The Landlord Academy

- **www.narpm.org** — National Association of Residential Property Managers

Ezine Articles on Property Management

- **www.ezinearticles.com**

- **www.Helium.com**

- **www.Searchwarp.com**

- **www.articlesbase.com**

Credit Bureaus

- **www.experian.com** — Experian Credit Bureau

- **www.transunion.com** — Transunion Credit Bureau

- **www.Equifax.com** — Equifax Credit Bureau

- **www.annualcreditreport.com** — Tenants can get a free copy of their credit report once a year.

Property Management Business Forms

- **www.pbp1.com** — Peachtree Business Products

- **www.ezlandlordforms.com** — Provides forms and a chat line for landlords

- **www.allbusiness.com** — All Business company

- **www.landlordeguide.com** — *The Complete Landlord®* *e-Guide*

Miscellaneous Web Sites

- **www.LandlordLocks.com** — Master key systems and locks

- **www.deltasociety.org** — Information on assistive animals

INDEX